I0825253

Gayan
Vadan
Nirtan

Hazrat Pir-o-Murshid Inayat Khan

Gayan Vadan Nirtan

Second Edition

Hazrat Inayat Khan

Sulūk Press
Richmond, Virginia

Published by Sulūk Press
112 East Cary Street, Richmond, Virginia 23219
sulukpress.com

Cover design by Sandra Lillydahl

ISBN 978-1-941810-55-2 hardcase
ISBN 978-1-941810-56-9 e-book

Names: Inayat Khan, 1882–1927, author. | Inayat Khan, Zia, 1971–, author of foreword.
Title: Gayan Vadan Nirtan
Description: Second Edition, Richmond, VA: Sulūk Press, 2026. | Includes foreword, biographical note, glossary, index.
Identifiers: LCCN 2015942149 | ISBN 9781941810552 (hardcase) | | ISBN 9781941810569 (e-book)
Subjects: LCSH: Sufism BISAC: Religion/Sufi | Religion/Mysticism | Poetry

Printed and bound in the United States of America

Contents

Foreword

If the twelve Message volumes represent the body of Hazrat Inayat Khan's Sufi teaching, the trilogy of *Gayan*, *Vadan*, and *Nirtan* form its beating heart. In the sayings, poems, and prayers that make up these three books, the very essence of the teacher's message is contained.

The sayings in this trilogy derive largely from Hazrat Inayat Khan's notebooks. It was the teacher's practice, as inspirations came, to inscribe them in little black books that he carried with him. From these inscriptions two collections were published in his lifetime, *Notes from the Unstruck Music from the Gayan* (1923) and *The Divine Symphony, or Vadan* (1926). After his death the trilogy was brought to completion with the publication of *Nirtan, or the Dance of the Soul* (1928).

Gayan, *Vadan*, and *Nirtan* share a common system of arrangement based on categories drawn from classical Indian music: *alapa*, *alankara*, *bola*, *chala*, *gamaka*, *gayatri*, *raga*, *sura*, *tala*, and *tana*. Hazrat Inayat Khan's mystical explanations of these terms appear at the beginning of each of the three volumes. These explanations vary somewhat from volume to volume, and *Nirtan* does not include the categories *alapa*, *gayatri*, and *raga*.

Hazrat Inayat Khan asked his students to preserve his words in their original form, saying, "If you will preserve my words as spoken, it will be as saving my life." The present edition of *Gayan, Vadan, Nirtan* honors this obligation by reversing subsequent changes and returning to Hazrat Inayat Khan's own phraseology. In doing so we have followed the findings of the Nekbakht Foundation, whose *Complete Works of Pir-o-Murshid Hazrat Inayat Khan* series establishes the teacher's original formulations. Many thanks are due to the Nekbakht Foundation for their meticulous work, without which this edition could not have been realized.

Hazrat Inayat Khan spoke the English of his time. A century later, conventions have changed. References to God as "He" and to humanity as "man," for example, now sound archaic. In responding to our current moment, such archaisms have been modified—using the minimalist approach to changes followed in the Centennial Edition—to make the sayings more inclusive and contemporary. In addition, sayings from the *Vadan* that were in the original publication and earlier versions but left out of the 2015 edition for lack of documentary evidence of their authenticity have been restored on the basis of further archival research. This includes the Golden, Silver, Copper, and Iron rules.

Gayan, Vadan, Nirtan is not an ordinary book. Hazrat Inayat Khan once said, "What is spoken from the heart reaches the heart." The sayings in *Gayan, Vadan, Nirtan* have come directly from the kindled heart and soul of Hazrat Inayat Khan. They are addressed to the deepest organs of feeling and knowing within us.

GAYAN

Notes from the Unstruck Music

Alapa: God speaking to humanity. This is the principal theme of the Message.

Alankara: The fanciful expression of an idea.

Bola: A kindled word.

Chala: An illuminated word.

Gamaka: The feeling of a poet's heart, keyed to various notes.

Gayatri: Prayer.

Raga: The human soul calling upon the Beloved God.

Sura: God speaking through the kindled soul.

Tala: The rhythmic expression of an idea.

Tana: The soul speaking with nature.

Alapas

When a glimpse of Our image is caught in the human,
When heaven and earth are sought in the human,
Then what is in the world that is not in the human?
If one only explored them, there's a lot in the human.

If you will go forward to find Us, We will come forward to receive you.

Give Us all you have, and We shall give you all We possess.

O peacemaker, before trying to make peace through the world, make peace within thyself.

Thou art the master of life here and in the hereafter.

Alankaras

Indifference, my most intimate friend, I am sorry, for I always have to act as thy opponent.

My modesty, thou art the thin veil that covereth subtle vanity.

My humility, thou art the very essence of vanity.

Vanity, both saint and sinner drink from thy cup.

Vanity, thou art the fountain of wine on the earth, where cometh the Sovereign of Heaven to drink.

Peacock, is it not thy vanity which causeth thee to dance?

My bare feet, step gently on the path of life, or else the thorns on the path that hurt you so will murmur among themselves, saying that you have thoughtlessly trampled upon them.

My ideal, I imagine at moments as if we were playing seesaw; when I rise up, thou goest down below my feet, and when I go down, thou risest above my head.

Self-dependence, thou makest me poor, but rich at the same time.

Wert thou not laughing under thy sleeves, my beloved ideal, when I was searching for thee on the earth?

My feeling heart, I so often wish you were made of a rock.

My limitation, thou art as a mote in the eye of my soul.

Money, thou art a bliss and a curse at the same time; thou turnest friends into foes and foes into friends; thou takest away and givest at the same time anxiety in life.

We are *apsaras* of heaven, when the
wind plays music we dance.
Earthly treasure is not our seeking,
our reward is Indra's one glance.

Time, I have never seen thee, but I have heard thy steps.

Time, in my sorrow thou creepest, in my joy thou runnest, in the hours of my patient waiting thou standest still.

Time, thou are the ocean, and every movement of life is thy wave.

Sky, thou art a sea wherein my imagination's boat sails.

My thoughtful self, reproach no one, hold a grudge against no one, take revenge with no one, bear malice against no one; be wise.

Be kind to all, tolerant to all, considerate to all, polite to all, O my thoughtful self.

My independent spirit, how many sacrifices I make for thy maintenance, and yet thou art never satisfied.

My simple trust, how often thou hast failed me. I still go on following you with my eyes closed.

Bolas

The whole of life's good deeds may be drowned in the flood caused by one single sin.

A wise person without willpower is as a head without a body.

All that one holds is conserved; all that one lets go is dispersed.

Pure conscience gives the strength of a lion, and by a guilty conscience even a lion turns into a rabbit.

The only condition of life is making one's own nature.

Be true or false, for you cannot be both.

The Truth is a divine inheritance found in the depth of the heart of every person.

A lifelong time is not sufficient to learn how to live in this world.

In poverty all evils breed.

When one touches the intimate Truth one realizes that there is nothing which is not in oneself.

Reason is the illusion of reality.

Lull the devil to sleep.

Movement is life; stillness is death.

It is not the action in itself that is sin or virtue; it is the condition that makes it either one or the other.

The Truth itself is its own evidence.

You cannot prove to be what in reality you are not.

You must not try to be what in reality you are not.

Pleasure blocks, but pain clears the way of inspiration.

Mystics do not wait till the hereafter but do all they can to progress just now.

Power demands subjection, but if you cannot fight the power, win it by surrender.

Human personality is a music that has a tone and rhythm of its own.

Take oneself to task instead of putting one's faults on others.

A human heart is the shell in which sincerity as a pearl is formed.

Love guides its own way.

People make their reasons to suit themselves.

Single-mindedness ensures success.

Love of form, progressing, culminates in love of the formless.

A worldly loss often turns into a spiritual gain.

The ideal is a means, but its breaking is the goal.

Many feel, but few think; and fewer there are who can express their thought.

The value of sacrifice is in willingness.

Refined manners with sincerity make a living art.

Longing for vengeance is like a craving for poison.

God is the central theme of the poet.
God is the portrait that the prophet paints.

True belief is independent of reason.

The more one knows, the more one finds there is to learn.

When a soul is attuned, its every action becomes a music.

Death is a tax that the soul has to pay for having had a name and a form.

The best way of living is to live a natural life.

To justify self for wrongdoing on the ground that another is guilty of the same fault is far from just.

Do not take the example of another as an excuse for your wrongdoings.

All the situations of life are tests to distinguish between the real and the false.

If you wish to follow the path of saints, first learn forgiveness.

Spare words if you wish your words to be powerful.

The gardener uses both roses in the flowerbed and thorns in making fences.

Love's best expression is indifference.

The unsociable person is a burden to the society.

Divinity is human perfection and divine limitation.

The wise show their admiration by respect.

Many admit the truth to themselves, but few confess it to others.

It is the twist of thought that is the curl of the Beloved.

Satan comes in most beautiful garbs to cover from the sight of humans their highest ideal.

Behind is one spirit and one life; how can we then be happy if our neighbors are not?

Nothing in the world is more valuable than every moment of your life.

Self-pity is the cause of all the grievances of life.

A gift of love is priceless.

It is our perception of time which passeth, time does not pass; time is God, and God is eternal.

The mystic begins by wondering at life.

The life of the mystic is a phenomenon at every moment.

In beauty is the secret of divinity.

Clean body reflects purity of the soul.
It is the purity of soul that gives a tendency to cleanliness.
Cleanliness is the secret of health.
Clean body signifies clean mind.
Purity of the soul is reflected in the cleanliness of body.
It is the pure in spirit who keep their body clean.

Reserve gives weight to the personality.

A serious and yet pleasant-spoken person is really honorable.

When soberness comes after the intoxication of life, one begins to wonder.

A life with a foolish companion is worse than death.

The pain of life is a price paid for the quickening of the heart.

By the power of endurance things become precious and people become great.

The heart closed to others means the heart closed to God.

Spirituality is the tuning of the heart; neither by study nor by piety can one attain it.

A person's morals must be judged from their attitude rather than from their action.

Reason is a flower with a thousand petals, one covered by another.

Fighting against nature is rising above nature.

Simplicity of nature is the sign of saints.

Life is full of blessings if one only knew how to have them.

Nothing false will succeed, and if it apparently succeeds it must only bring false benefit.

All that produces longing in the heart deprives the heart of its freedom.

It is the exaltation of the spirit that is productive of all beauty.

One virtue can take a stand against a thousand vices.

Consideration is born in the heart and is developed in the head.

Life is distinguished by the pairs of opposites.

There is nothing in this life's fair that we shall take and will not have to pay for.

A diamond must be cut before its light can shine out.

Beyond goodness is trueness, which is a divine quality.

A guilty conscience robs the will of its power.

The answer that uproots the question from its ground is the answer of the truly inspired one.

Trust in others is of no value if one has no trust in oneself.

Love develops into harmony, and in harmony is born beauty.

Devotion is proved by sacrifice.

In nature it is God who by human hands designs and carries out God's intended plans.

The word that is not heard is lost.

Consideration is the sign of the wise.

One's attitude is manifest in the expression of one's countenance.

Sin is the fuel for virtue's fire.

The first lesson that the seeker after truth must learn is to be true to oneself.

Subtlety is the art of intelligence.

People build four walls around their ideas, lest their ideas may escape their imprisonment.

Love rises in emotion and falls in passion.

The whole trend of life is a journey from imperfection to perfection.

Every soul has its own way in life; if you walk another person's way, you must borrow that person's eyes.

One's personality reflects one's thought and deed.

Reason is learned from the ever-changing world, but knowledge comes from the essence of life.

The domain of the mystic is the self, over which he or she is ruler.

If one would become straightforward, certainly a straight way would be opened before one.

No one can be human and not make a mistake.

Humility of conscience dims the radiance of the countenance.

The desire to develop one's personality is the real purpose of human life.

People express their soul in everything they do.

When the heart breaks it gives birth to the soul.

There is no better companion than solitude.

Life is what it is; you cannot change it, but you can change yourself.

The word is living, but the silence is life.

Who keeps no secrets, has no depth in their heart.

The heart that cannot keep secret is like a vessel upside down.

Wisdom is attained in solitude.

There is no desire in the world that has no answer. If this philosophy were wrong, the creation would not exist.

If in Truth we shall not build our hope, in what shall we build?

The admirer of nature is the true worshipper of God.

Love that depends not on reciprocity stands upon its own feet.

Patient endurance is the strongest means of defense.

All that is really worthwhile is difficult to attain.

It is not the situation in life, but it is one's attitude toward life that makes one happy or unhappy.

Gain by the loss of another is not profitable in the end.

Talking wisdom is much easier than living it.

Charity is the expansion of the heart.

God is the answer to every question.

Make ye God a reality, and God will make you the Truth.

God made humans, and humans made good or bad.

Give all you have and take all you are given.

The Creator is lost in the Creator's own creation.

Natural religion is the religion of beauty.

All surrender to beauty willingly and to power unwillingly.

The creation is not only the nature of God but also God's art.

Vanity is the impetus hidden behind almost every impulse.

Vanity brings out the best and worst in people.

Time and space are but the divisions of the infinite.

Vanity is the sum total of every living activity in the world.

A charming personality is gold with perfume.

A dancing soul expresses its rapture through all its expressions.

A beautiful personality is as a beautiful piece of art with life in it.

The Holy Mother was the stepping stone for Jesus toward Christhood.

Muhammad's sword was the charm of his personality.

When the personality of an artist is absorbed in his or her art it becomes art itself.

Vanity is the mask over the object that draws every soul.

Vanity is the crown of beauty and modesty its throne.

Nature is the very being of humans; therefore, they feel at one with nature.

In the country you can see God's glory, and in the city you can glorify God's name.

The true art does not take one away from nature; on the contrary, it brings one closer to it.

A person without character is as a flower without perfume.

Love is a net in which hearts are caught as fishes.

While everyone in the world asks "Why?" of their neighbors, mystics ask this question of themselves.

A human being is pulled from four sides in life: by the ideal, nature, circumstances, and law.

A child born on earth is an exile from heaven.

No tie can bind if your heart is free.

Great personalities are few, and fewer still are those who can recognize and appreciate them.

No person living on earth can come up to your ideal except a hero from a story of the past.

The one whom you expect to be your ideal will prove to be your ideal someday when he or she has gone past.

The true ego is born of the ashes of the false ego.

If by accident you step in the mud, it is not necessary to keep on the muddy path.

Matter is a state of spirit.

A living word is life itself.

Sympathy breaks the congestion of the heart.

An action is a reaction of thought.

Reason is the master of the unbeliever and the slave of the believer.

When desire abides in a steady thought it ensures success.

No sacrifice is ever too great to be offered to the cause of liberty.

The fruitless life is a useless life.

Gold is that which proves to be real to the end of the test.

To make God intelligible you have to make a God.

Truth alone can succeed falsehood, and falsehood is the waste of time and loss of energy.

What begins with deception continues in it and ends in the same.

The wise says in one word what the foolish cannot explain in a thousand words.

Burning words rise from a glowing heart.

One's own attitude becomes an obstacle on the path of the pessimist.

The shortage of patience starves virtue to death.

The seeming death is the real birth of the soul.

Truth that disturbs peace and harmony is worse than a lie.

It takes a thousand lies to prove one false statement true, and yet in the end it must prove false.

The way of the Sufi is to experience life and yet to keep above it.

Live in the world but do not become of it.

Life is opportunity, not only to accomplish what one desires but even to fulfill what one's soul yearns for.

Nobleness of character is an inborn quality as fragrance in the flower; it cannot be taught or learned.

One word of the truly inspired one answers a hundred questions and avoids a thousand unnecessary words of explanation.

Every moment of life is an opportunity, and the greatest opportunity is to know the value of opportunity.

It is the spirit of discipleship that opens the vision.

You must find your ideal in yourself. If no one comes up to your ideal, you must make one.

Through matter the soul attains to its highest realization.

If a desire is not fulfilled, it means that the person did not know how to desire.

Failure is caused by indistinctness of motive.

The charming personality of the prophet is a divine net in which God captures the souls drifting in the world.

A clever person with a biting tongue is like a serpent with its poisonous teeth.

We each create our God—but God's form, not God's life.

We each picture God in the form we imagine, thus making many gods out of the one single Being.

God alone exists, as many gods or as one God, for two means only twice one.

Chalas

The spiritual guide performs the role of Cupid in bringing the seeking souls closer to God.

The same light that is fire on earth and the sun in the sky is God in heaven.

It is presumption on the part of humans when they demand in words an explanation of God.

The beauty that modesty covers, art discovers gently; while respecting the human tendency, it unveils beauty that human convention hides.

God lives in nature and is buried alive under the artificial forms that stand covering God as God's graves.

The good reputation is as fragile as a glass.

The good reputation is a trust given to one from people, and it is the sacred duty of a person to prove worthy of this trust.

Take great care of your reputation, if you at all care for it.

The person who has no reputation has no feeling for the reputation of another.

People inherit from their ancestors not only their body but their mind also.

The wretched look for some excuse to be miserable.

You must never make fun with fools; if you will throw a flower at them in fun, they will throw at you a stone.

The alchemy is in the stilling of the heart, when mercury becomes silver.

A real success is proved by its durability.

Stand through life as firm as a rock in the sea, undisturbed and unmoved by its ever-rising waves.

Discovering of error is uncovering of light.

The truth spoken sincerely certainly must carve the heart.

Spiritual attainment is the true purpose of every soul.

The more people you can get on with, the wiser person you are.

Do you wish for a relief in life? Rise above complexity and conventionality.

It does not matter what you have lost, so long as your soul is not lost.

One single moment of truthful life is worth more than a thousand years of a life in falsehood.

Worrying about the faults of others is an extra worry in addition to the worry that comes from one's own faults.

Success gives a real appearance even to false things.

No one can sustain inharmony in life, though many ignorantly maintain it.

All things in their beginnings must be guarded from the sweeping wind of destruction, as small plants must be nurtured in a glass house.

It is ignorant believers who cause a revolt in an intelligent person by their claim of belief, thereby turning that person into an unbeliever.

A selfish person cannot imagine anyone being unselfish.

The selfish always suspects the unselfish of falsehood.

God's majesty is seen in nature, but God's scantiness in the grandeur of human life.

It takes but a moment to drop down from heaven to earth, but a lifetime may not be sufficient to rise from the earth to heaven.

If you walk through light and yet seek the path of darkness, it is like being pulled by the two poles of the world; you are torn between the two, neither can you go one way nor the other.

Joy and sorrow both are for each other: if it were not for joy, sorrow would not be; and if it were not for sorrow, joy would not be experienced.

People wonder about their past and future; how wonderful would life become for them if they only realized the eternal now.

The spirit of discipleship is most necessary in one's journey along the spiritual path.

When it is so very difficult to prove truth to be true, how much more difficult must it be to prove true that which is false.

Purgatory is a state that mind experiences between the birth of thought and its materialization.

It is the darkness of your own heart that, falling on the heart of another, becomes a doubt in him or her.

Truth conceived by the mature soul is expressed as wisdom.

Goodness and wickedness both exist in human nature—the only difference is when one is manifest to view, the other is hidden like a lining inside the coat.

The physical body is a necessity for the fulfillment of the purpose of the soul.

Absence of generosity means that the doors of the heart are closed.

Passing through an evolution on earth is necessary for the spirit to arrive at its culmination.

A sarcastic remark can be more hurtful than a scorpion's sting.

Let not your reputation fall in the hands of the monkeys; they will look at it curiously, mock at it, laugh at it, and snatch it from each other's hands. In the end they will tear it to pieces.

Do not entrust the devil with your secrets; if you do so, then the one who is meant to be your slave will become your master.

With goodwill and trust in God, with self-confidence and a hopeful attitude in life, one will always win one's battle, however difficult.

All things existing have their opposites save God. It is therefore that God cannot be made intelligible to the unbeliever.

Truth is purifying, truth is most lovable, truth is peace-giving, but what is truth? Truth is what you cannot speak.

If your fellow humans do not pay you their debt, forbear patiently; some day it will be paid back to you to every farthing, together with its interest.

Heaven and hell are the material manifestation of agreeable or disagreeable thoughts.

It is for the consideration of his subjects that the king has to abide by the law; if not, the king is above law.

What man makes is the personality of God, not God's reality.

Many evils are born of riches, but many more still breed in poverty.

The spirit of controversy lives on argument.

Death is preferable to asking favor of a small person.

Let the devil sleep rather than be awake.

A biting tongue goes deeper than the point of a bayonet.

Cutting words pierce deeper than a poisoned sword.

Human character may be likened to metal: if you wish to make anything out of metal, you must melt it. So the human heart must be melted before it can be made into a desirable character.

The fountain stream of love rises in the love for an individual, but spreads and falls down in universal love.

A tenderhearted sinner is better than one who is hardened by piety.

The way to get over one's error is to admit one's fault first and then to refrain from falling into it again.

By accusing a person of a fault, you only make that person firm in it.

When envy develops into jealousy, the heart turns from sour to bitter.

One who is a riddle to another is a puzzle to him- or herself.

When misers show any generosity, they celebrate it with trumpets.

Sincere people have a fragrance about them that a sincere heart perceives.

If you are not able to control your thought, you cannot hold it.

It is the spirit of hopelessness that blocks one's path and prevents one's advancement.

Sincerity is like a bud in the heart of a person, and it blossoms with the maturity of the soul.

No one will experience in life that which is not meant for him or her.

It is impossible to only be praised and not be blamed. Praise and blame go together, hand in hand.

To be in uncongenial surroundings is worse than being in one's grave.

Science is born of the seed of intuition, conceived in reason.

Truth alone is success, and the real success is the truth.

When the cry of the disciple has reached a certain pitch, the teacher comes to answer it.

People who are difficult to deal with are difficult to themselves.

It is sympathy rather than food that will satisfy your guest.

The person who is not courageous enough to take risks will not accomplish anything.

As the flower is the forerunner of the fruit, so one's childhood is the promise of one's life.

Do not offend a low person; it is like throwing a stone in the mud and getting splashes upon oneself.

The self-made person is greater than the one who depends on another to make him or her.

False politeness is like imitation jewelry.

Do not accept that which you cannot return, for the balance of life is in reciprocity.

Those whom their individuality fails, seek their refuge in community.

Taking the path of inharmony is like entering the mouth of the dragon.

Life is an opportunity; it is a great pity that people realize this when it is already too late.

Love is the Divine Mother's arms; and when those arms are outspread, every soul falls into them.

The greatest tragedy of the world is the lack of general evolution.

There is nothing to be surprised at in life; all situations of life work toward some definite end.

Forgiveness belongs to God; it becomes the privilege of mortals only when asked by another.

Every moment of life is a precious moment.

People learn their first lesson of love by loving a human being, but in reality love is due to God alone.

You need not look for a saint or a master; a wise person is sufficient to guide your path.

Those who cannot learn their lesson by their first fault in life are certainly on the wrong track.

Overlook the greatest fault of another, but do not partake of it in the smallest degree.

The fulfillment of every activity is in its balance.

The human heart is a temple; when its door is closed to another it is also closed to God.

Success is achieved when free will and circumstances work hand in hand.

Every impression of a bad happening should be met with a combative attitude.

Those guilty of the same fault unite in making a virtue out of their common sin.

Wickedness that manifests from the intelligent person is like a poisonous fruit coming out of a fertile ground.

A joke tickles the intelligence and clears away the clouds of gloom from the heart.

Service of God means we each work for all.

If you wish to probe the depths of a person's character, test that person with wine, wealth, or romance.

It is the lack of personal magnetism that makes a person look for magnetic objects.

Fire can cook food or burn it; so is the effect of pain upon the human heart.

Every desire increases a power by which one can accomplish one's main desire, which is the desire of every soul.

Every experience, good or bad, is a step forward in one's evolution in life.

It is no use saying, "I know the truth"; if you knew the truth, you would keep silent.

Human suffering is the first call we have to answer.

It is easy to become a teacher but difficult to become a pupil.

As poison acts as nectar in some cases, so in certain situations evil proves to be a virtue.

To find apt words to express one's thoughts is like making a good shot.

Those who realize the effect of their deed upon themselves commence to open their outlook on life.

What humans make God breaks; what God makes humans destroy.

All things are good, but they are not good for every person nor right for all times.

The false ego is a false god; when the false god is destroyed, the true God comes.

When a person does not listen to us, we must know that it comes from this: that we ourselves do not believe.

The common disease is considered as normal health by the generality.

Love in its beginning can only live on reciprocity, but when developed can stand on its own feet.

The present spirit of humanity has commercialism as its crown and materialism as its throne.

Without humor life is empty.

To see life as a whole is beyond the power of the generality.

No object or life can exist that has not one central point in which everything meets and joins together, and that meeting ground is called the Divine Mind.

The more you make of your gifts, the less becomes the value of something that is priceless.

The secret of life is balance, and the absence of balance is life's destruction.

Gamakas

I consider myself second to none since I have realized in myself the One Alone.

All things that may seem to you to be exalting my position, indeed lower me in my eyes; the only thing exalting for me is the forgetting of myself entirely in the perfect vision of God.

There is nothing that I consider too good for me or too high to attain to; on the contrary, all possible attainments seem within my reach since I have attained to the vision of my Lord.

There is nothing that I feel too humiliated to do, and there is no position, however exalted, that can make me feel prouder than what I am already in the pride of the Lord.

Neither does love exalt nor hate depress me, for all things to me seem natural. Life for me is a dream that changeth constantly, and when I withdraw my real self from the false, I know all things and yet stand remote; so I rise above all changes of life.

It makes no difference to me if I am so praised that I am raised from earth to heaven, or if I am so blamed that I am thrown from the greatest heights to the depths of the earth. Life to me is an ever-moving sea in which the waves of favor and disfavor constantly rise and fall.

A fall does not break or discourage me; it only raises me to a new life.

I could not have enjoyed virtue's beauty if I had not known sin.

Every loss in life I consider as the throwing off of an old garment in order to put on a new one; and the new garment has always been better than the old one.

I have learned more by my faults than by my merits. If I acted always aright, I could not be human.

My intuition never fails me, but I fail whenever I do not listen to my intuition.

Patience is the lesson I had from the moment I stepped on the earth; ever since, I have tried to practice it, but more there is to be learned.

I blame no one for their wrongdoing; neither do I encourage them in that direction.

In bringing happiness to others I feel the pleasure of God, and for my inadvertence I feel myself blameworthy before God.

Every soul stands before me as a world, and the light of my spirit falling upon it brings clearly to my view all it contains.

Nothing seems to me either too good or too bad; I know no distinction anymore between saint and sinner since I behold the one single life manifested in all.

My action toward every person I consider as my action toward God, and the action of every person toward me I take as an action of God.

As long as I act upon my own intuition, I succeed, but whenever I follow the advice of others I go astray.

I work simply, not troubling about results. My satisfaction is in accomplishing the work that is given to me to my best ability, and I leave the effect to the Cause.

Life in the world is most interesting, but solitude away from this world is never enough for me.

I feel myself when I am by myself.

By respecting every person I meet I worship God.

In loving every soul on earth I feel my devotion to God.

There is nothing else in life that pleases me more than pleasing others, but it is difficult to please everybody.

I am ready to learn from those who come to teach me and willing to teach those who wish to learn.

I regard every failure as a stepping stone toward a success.

I will have heaven or hell but not purgatory.

I do not intend to teach my fellow humans, but to show them all I see.

At the moment when I shall be leaving this earth, it is not the number of followers that will make me proud; it is the thought that I have delivered God's message to some souls that will console me, and the feeling that it helped them through life that will bring me satisfaction.

Hail to my exile from the Garden of Eden to the earth; if I had not fallen, I would not have probed the depths of life.

I have not come to change humanity; I have come to help it on.

If anyone throws it down, my heart does not break, it bursts, and the flame coming rises from it, which becomes my torch.

My deep sigh rises above as a cry of the earth, and an answer comes from within as a message.

I am a tide in the sea of life, bearing toward the shore all who come within my enfoldment.

Gayatris

Saum

Praise be to Thee, Most Supreme God,
Omnipotent, Omnipresent, All-pervading,
the Only Being.
Take us in Thy Parental Arms,
raise us from the denseness of the earth.
Thy Beauty do we worship,
to Thee do we give willing surrender.
Most Merciful and Compassionate God,
the Idealized Sovereign of the whole humanity,
Thee only do we worship,
and toward Thee alone do we aspire.
Open our hearts toward Thy Beauty,
illuminate our souls with Divine Light.
O Thou, the Perfection of Love, Harmony, and Beauty!
All-powerful Creator, Sustainer, Judge, and Forgiver of our shortcomings,
Sovereign God of the East and of the West,
of the worlds above and below,
and of the seen and unseen beings.
Pour upon us Thy Love and Thy Light,
give sustenance to our bodies, hearts, and souls,
use us for the purpose that Thy Wisdom chooseth,
and guide us on the path of Thine Own Goodness.
Draw us closer to Thee every moment of our life,
until in us be reflected Thy Grace,
Thy Glory, Thy Wisdom, Thy Joy, and Thy Peace.
Amen.

Salat

Most gracious Sovereign,
Messenger, Messiah, and Savior of humanity,
we greet Thee with all humility.
Thou art the First Cause and the Last Effect,
the Divine Light and the Spirit of Guidance,
Alpha and Omega.
Thy Light is in all forms,
Thy Love in all beings:
in a loving mother, in a kind father, in an innocent child,
in a helpful friend, in an inspiring teacher.
Allow us to recognize Thee in all Thy holy names and forms:
as Rama, as Krishna, as Shiva, as Buddha.
Let us know Thee as Abraham, as Solomon, as Zarathustra,
as Moses, as Jesus, as Muhammad,
and in many other names and forms, known and unknown to the world.
We adore Thy Past,
Thy Presence deeply enlightens our being,
and we look for Thy blessing in the future.
O Messenger, Christ, Nabi, the Rasul of God!
Thou Whose heart constantly reaches upward,
Thou comest on earth with a message,
as a dove from above, when Dharma decays,
and speakest the Word that is put into Thy mouth,
as the light filleth the crescent moon.
Let the star of the Divine Light shining in Thy heart
be reflected in the hearts of Thy devotees.
May the Message of God reach far and wide,
illuminating and making the whole humanity
as one single family in the Parenthood of God.
Amen.

Khatum

O Thou, Who art the Perfection of Love, Harmony, and Beauty,
the Sovereign of heaven and earth,
open our hearts, that we may hear Thy Voice,
which constantly cometh from within.
Disclose to us Thy Divine Light,
which is hidden in our souls,
that we may know and understand life better.
Most Merciful and Compassionate God,
give us Thy great Goodness,
teach us Thy loving Forgiveness,
raise us above the distinctions and differences which divide us,
send us the Peace of Thy Divine Spirit,
and unite us all in Thy Perfect Being.
Amen.

Dowa

Save me, my Sovereign, from the earthly passions and
the attachments which blind humanity.
Save me, my Sovereign, from the temptations of power, fame,
and wealth, which keep us away from Thy glorious vision.
Save me, my Sovereign, from the souls who are constantly
occupied in hurting and harming their fellow people, and who
take pleasure in the pain of another.
Save me, my Sovereign, from the evil eye of envy and jealousy,
which falleth upon Thy bountiful gifts.
Save me, my Sovereign, from falling into the hands of the
playful children of earth, lest they might use me in their games;
they might play with me and then break me in the end, as
children destroy their toys.
Save me, my Sovereign, from all manner of injury that cometh
from the bitterness of my adversaries and from the ignorance of
my loving friends.
Amen.

Nayaz

Beloved Sovereign, Almighty God!
Through the rays of the sun,
through the waves of the air,
through the All-pervading Life in space,
purify and revivify me, and, I pray,
heal my body, heart, and soul.
Amen.

Nazar

O Thou, the Sustainer of our bodies, hearts, and souls,
bless all that we receive in thankfulness.
Amen.

Ragas

Thy light hath illuminated the dark chamber of my mind;
Thy love is rooted in the depth of my heart.
Thine ears are attached to my heart;
Thine eyes are the sight of my soul.
Thy power works behind my action;
Thy peace is alone the repose in my life.
Thy will works behind my every impulse;
Thy voice speaketh my words.
Thine own image is my countenance;
My body covereth Thy soul.
My life is Thy very breath, my Beloved,
And my self is Thine own Being.

Thou pourest wine into my empty cup wherever we meet,
    on hills and dales, on the top of the high mountains,
    in the thick forests and in the barren deserts,
    on the shores of the roaring sea and on the banks of the
    gentle river;
And there ariseth in my heart the unearthly passion
    and the heavenly joy.

Thou hast won my heart a thousand times over again.
Thou comest veiled under many and varied guises,
    and in every guise Thou art unique.

Who is not deluded by the splendor Thou hast so skillfully
produced on the face of the earth?
In this beauty fair Thou shinest, adorned in myriad garbs.
Thine own is all the beauty, and it is Thou Thyself
who art attracted by it.
Thou on the stage of life actest as friend, as foe,
and Thou alone seest this play performed so wonderfully.
I sought Thee so long, my Beloved, and now I have found
Thee at last, O Winner of my heart, and in finding Thee
I have lost myself.

Let me feel Thine arms around me, Beloved,
while I am wandering away from home.
Let my heart become Thy lute.
Hearing Thy song my soul cometh to life.
Let my virgin soul dance at Thy court, my Indra;
the passion it hath is for Thee alone.
O let me lean my head on Thy breast,
Thine arms enfolding me, my feet touch paradise.

Wherever I look, I see Thy beloved face covered under
many different veils.
The magic power of my ever-seeking eyes lifted the veil
from Thy glowing countenance, and Thy sweet smiles
win my heart a thousand times over.
The luster of Thy piercing glance hath lighted my darkened soul,
and lo, now I see the sun shine everywhere.

On the bright, sunny day and in the darkness of night,
what didst Thou not teach me!
Thou hast taught me what is meant by wrong
and what is called right.
Thou hast shown me the hideous face of life, and Thou hast

unveiled before me life's beautiful countenance.
Thou hast taught me wisdom out of utter darkness of ignorance.
Thou hast taught me to think after my thoughtless hours.
And Thou playest with me, my Beloved Liege and Messenger,
hide-and-seek.
Thou didst close my eyes, and Thou hast opened them.

When we are face-to-face, Beloved, I do not know whether
to call Thee me, or me Thee.
I see my self when Thou art not before me; when I see Thee,
my self is lost to my view.
I consider it a great fortune when Thou art alone with me,
but when I am not at all there, I think it the greatest luck.

Thy whispering to the ears of my heart moveth my soul to ecstasy.
The waves of joy that rise in my heart make a swing for
Thy living word.
My heart patiently awaiteth Thy word, deaf to all that
calleth from without.
O Thou, who art enshrined in my heart, speak some more:
Thy voice exalteth my soul.

When Thou art before me, my Beloved,
I rise upon wings and my burden becometh light;
but when my little self riseth before my eyes
I drop to the earth, and all its weight falleth upon me.

My soul is moved to dance by the charm of Thy graceful
movements, and my heart beateth the rhythm
of Thy gentle steps.
The sweet impression of Thy winning countenance,
my worshipped One, covereth all visible things from my
sight.

My heart re-echoes the melody Thou playest on Thy flute,
and it bringeth my soul in harmony with the whole universe.

I dare not think of raising my eyes to look at Thy glorious vision.
I quietly sit by the lake of my heart, watching in it
Thy most lovely image reflected.

Thou givest me Thine own love and Thou winnest my heart
with the charm of Thy beauty.
When I approach thee fondly, my Beloved, Thou sayest to me:
"Touch me not!"

I cling to Thee with a child's faith,
bearing in my heart Thy most lovely image.
I have sought refuge under Thy bosom, Beloved,
and I am safe, feeling Thine arms around me.

How shall I thank Thee, my Sovereign, for Thy bountiful gifts?
Every gift Thou givest me, my generous Liege, is invaluable.
A tongue of flame arose out of the twinkling spark of my heart
by Thy gentle blowing.
Thou hast opened the ears of my heart that I may hear
Thy softest whisper.
Thou hast taught me Thine own tongue and to read the characters
written by Thy pen.

I call Thee my Sovereign when I am conscious of my bubble-like self; but when I am conscious of Thee, my Beloved, I call Thee me.

How shall I thank Thee for Thy mercy and compassion,
O Sovereign of my soul?

What didst Thou not do for me when I was walking alone
through the wilderness, through the darkness of night?
Thou didst come with Thy lighted torch and didst
illuminate my path.
Frozen with the coldness of the world's hardness of heart,
I sought refuge in Thee, and Thou didst console me
with Thine endless love.
I knocked at Thy gate at last when I had no answer
from anywhere in the world,
and Thou didst answer readily my broken heart's call.

I searched and searched and searched,
and I could not find Thee anywhere.
I called Thee aloud, standing on the minaret.
I rang the temple bell with the rising and setting of the sun.
I bathed in the Ganges in vain.
I came back from Ka'ba disappointed.
I looked for Thee on the earth, and I searched for Thee in heaven,
my Beloved, my Pearl, but at last I have found Thee
hidden in the shell of my heart.

I would willingly die a thousand deaths if by dying
I could attain Thy most lofty presence.
If it were a cup of poison Thy beloved hand offered,
I would prefer that poison to the bowl of nectar.
I value the dust under Thy feet, my Precious One,
most of all the treasures the earth holds.
If my head could touch the earth of Thy dwelling place,
I would proudly refuse Khusrau's crown.
I would gladly sacrifice all pleasures the earth can offer me,
if I could only retain the pain I have in my feeling heart.

One moment's life lived with Thee is worth more than a life of long years lived in Thine absence.

Give me one more cup, O Saki, which I will value more than the whole life I have lived.

My lifelong sorrow I forget when Thou casteth one glance o'er me. Time is not for me; a glimpse of Thy glorious vision maketh me eternal.

It is Thou who art my pride; when I realize my limited self, I feel myself the humblest of all living beings.

O Thou, the root of my life's plant, Thou wert hidden so long in my bud-like soul, but now thou hast come out, O my life's fruit, after the blossoming of my heart.

Let me grow quietly in Thy garden as a speechless plant, that some day my flowers and fruits might sing the legend of my silent past.

Thy music causeth my soul to dance.
In the cooing of the wind I hear Thy trumpet, and through
the gentle breeze cometh to my ears the music of Thy flute.
The waves in the sea keep the rhythm of my dancing steps.
In the voice of the thunder I hear Thy drums, and the lightning
playeth to me the music of cymbals.
Through the whole of nature I hear Thy music played, my Beloved,
and my soul while dancing, speaketh of its joy in song.

Thy smiling eyes have brought my dead heart to life again.
My life and death depend upon the closing and disclosing of
Thy magic glance.

Suras

Blessed are they who have found in life their life's purpose.

Blessed are they who rest in the abode of their soul.

Blessed are they who hear the call from the minaret of their heart.

Blessed are they who see the star of their soul as the light seen from the sea.

Blessed are the innocent who believe and trust simply.

Blessed are the unselfish friends whose motto in life is constancy.

Blessed are they who strive in the path of truth patiently.

Blessed are they who make willing sacrifices in kindness.

Blessed are they who cover the holes of others even from their own eyes.

Blessed are they who fear that they might hurt another by their thought or word or deed.

Blessed are the proud in God, for they shall inherit the kingdom of heaven.

Verily, the heart that reflecteth the divine Light is illuminated.

Verily, the heart that is respondent to the divine Word is liberated.

Verily, the heart that receiveth the divine Peace is blessed.

Verily, the heart that repeateth the sacred Name is exalted.

Verily, the heart that cherisheth the love of God will be crowned with that divine glory on the last day.

Enviable is one who loveth and asketh for no return.

Verily, it is truth that every soul is seeking.

Verily, the one who is hopeful will succeed in life.

Verily, life is one continual battle, and they alone are victorious who have conquered themselves.

Verily, all that leads to happiness is good.

Verily, one is pious who considers human feeling.

For every unfoldment there is a certain time, so there comes a time for the unfoldment of the soul.

The period of one's spiritual development depends upon the rhythm of one's life.

All things that one seeks in God, such as light, life, strength, joy and peace—these all can be found in truth. Verily, God is Truth.

Truth is the light that illuminates the whole life.

Truth is the evidence of God, and God is the evidence of Truth.

In the light of Truth all things become clear; their true nature manifests to view.

When one closes one's lips, God begins to speak.

There is no teacher save God; we all learn from God.

The consciousness of the one whole is the flesh of Christ, and the breath of love is his blood.

If the Almighty God chooseth, God hath power sufficient to turn thy shield into a poisoned sword and even thine own hand into the arm of thine adversary.

Your great enemies are those who are near and dear to you, but your still greater enemy is your own self.

Out of space arose light, and by that light space became illuminated.

Put your trust in God for support, and see God's hidden hand working through all sources.

People look for wonders; if they only saw how very wonderful is the human heart.

Do not cry with the crying ones, but console them; if not, by your sympathy you will make them cry more.

One word can be more precious than all the treasures of the earth.

The one who maketh room in the heart will find accommodation everywhere.

External life is but the shadow of the inner reality.

The secret of all success is the strength of conviction.

Those who try to make virtues out of their faults grope further and further into the darkness.

Patient endurance is the sign of progress.

Do not fear God, but regard carefully God's pleasure and displeasure.

Temptation is that which detains one on one's journey to the desired goal.

Fatality is one side of the truth, not all.

O righteous one, keep your goodness distant that it may not touch your sense of vanity.

The great teachers of humanity become streams of love.

One whose love has been reciprocated has not known what is love.

Faith ensures success.

The key to all happiness is the love of God.

As the shadow is apparent and yet nonexistent, so is evil.

To know the justice of God, you must be just yourself.

To whom the soul truly belongs, to that One in the end it returns.

In order to realize perfection one must lose one's imperfect self in the perfection of God.

The hereafter is the continuity of the same life in another sphere.

Those who live with God look to God for guidance at every move they make.

Independence and indifference are as two wings that enable the soul to fly.

Resignation is no good except in cases where a thing is done and it can't be helped.

Learn to live a true life and you will know the truth.

The world itself becomes a scripture or book to the soul.

One is an unbeliever who cannot believe him- or herself.

A pure life and clear conscience are as two eyes for the soul.

Righteousness comes from the essence of every soul.

When our self does not belong to us, what else can belong to us?

There is no source of happiness other than the human heart.

Faithfulness has a fragrance to it that is perceived in the atmosphere of the faithful.

One who does not recognize God—sooner or later God will make that one recognize God.

As soon as you knock at the gate of God, which is your heart, from there the answer comes.

There is no greater phenomenon than love itself.

Life is full of blessings if we only knew how to receive them.

Where the body goes, there the shadow will also go; so is truth followed by falsehood.

Life in the world is false, and its lovers revel in falsehood.

Faith means a living trust.

Faith in self must culminate in faith in God.

The sunglass reflects the heart of the sun; the contemplative heart reflects the divine qualities.

The soul is either raised or cast down by the power of its own thoughts, speech, and action.

Every soul seeks after beauty, and every virtue, righteousness, or good action is nothing but a glimpse of beauty.

To be alone by oneself is like being with a friend whose company will last forever.

It is the tongue of flame which speaketh the truth, not the tongue of flesh.

The one to whom life's purpose is clear is already on the path.

All that is precious we naturally hide; so the truth is hidden in the heart of nature.

We give a way to our faults by being passive to them.

The more one explores oneself, the more power one finds within oneself, which one could never have realized otherwise.

The ideal is the flower of the creation, and the realization of Truth is its fragrance.

The secret of the whole Creation is the hidden desire of the Creator.

The soul of Christ is the life of the universe.

The possessor of wealth is often a gatekeeper of his or her treasure house.

The words that enlighten are more precious than jewels.

Faith touches what reason fails to reach.

The whole world's treasure is too small a price for a word that kindles the soul.

Of what use is your sense, O sensible one, if it came to mourn over the opportunity you have lost?

If you will fail yourself, everybody will fail you.

If you are the master of your own domain, you certainly are the ruler of the world.

Means sufficient for the simple needs of everyday life are a greater boon than the riches that add to life's struggle.

In order to bring ourselves up to our ideal, we must first realize our own follies; next we must try to become better, believing that we can change.

When it is difficult even for the worldly people to live in the world, how much more difficult must it be for the godly.

When one has to choose between one's spiritual and material profit, then one shows whether one's treasure is on earth or in heaven.

Love is inexpressible in its fullness, but it is a power that speaks louder than words.

There is nothing that one is too weak to do when love's power gushes forth from one's heart.

Spiritual attainment is tuning oneself to a high pitch.

Unless you respect your own ideal, others will not respect it.

Believe in your own ideal first if you wish others to believe it.

The one who will attain power, not knowing its proper use, will lose it in the end with a considerable loss.

Power most often costs more than it is worth.

All that is held under power must some day revolt.

People show themselves to be greater or smaller according to the importance they attach to greater or smaller things in life.

There is nothing on earth or in heaven that is not within one's reach; when God is within one's reach, what else could be out of one's reach?

In faith is the secret of fulfillment or nonfulfillment of every thought.

Self-confidence is the true meaning of faith.

There is a limit to the precautions one takes in one's life's affairs, and that limit is one's trust in God.

The one who walks through life regardless of success, success pursues; the one who pursues success in life, success eludes.

Some are masters of success and some are its slaves.

There are two kinds among the seekers of God: one makes God, and the other mars.

Every thought, speech, and action that is natural, sound, and living is a virtue; and that which lacks the same is sin.

Talas

Silence serves: as a lock on the lips of the excitable;
as a barrier between two hearts severed from one another;
as a shield for the wise amidst fools; and
as a veil over the face of the unlettered before the well-versed.

Love from above is forgiveness,
from below is devotion,
from within is kindness, and
from without is affection.

One who returns more good for less good is a good person.
One who returns less good for more good is selfish.
One who tries to be even in the exchange of good is a practical
person.
But the one who returns good for evil is a saint.

One who returns less evil for more evil is ordinary.
One who tries to be even in returning evil is wicked.
One who returns more evil for less evil is cruel.
But the one who returns evil for good, for that one there is no
name.

Those who guard themselves against being fooled by another are
clever.
Those who do not allow another to fool them are wise.
Those who are fooled by another are simpletons.
But those who knowingly allow themselves to be fooled show
the character of the saint.

If you wish people to obey you,
you must learn to obey yourself.
If you wish people to believe you,
you must learn to believe yourself.
If you wish people to respect you,
you must learn to respect yourself.
If you wish people to trust you,
you must learn to trust yourself.

One proves to be genuine by one's sincerity.
One proves to be noble by one's charity of heart.
One proves to be wise by one's tolerance, and
one proves to be great by one's endurance
through the constantly jarring influences of life.

One is brave who courageously experiences all things.
One is a coward who is afraid to take a step in a new direction.
One is foolish who swims with tides of fancy and pleasure.
One is wise who experiences all things, yet keeps on the path
that leads one to one's destination.

The warden of the prison is in a worse position than the prisoners themselves; while the bodies of the prisoners are in captivity, the mind of the warden is in prison.

For all you take in this world you must pay a price. For some things you must pay in advance, for some things you should pay on delivery, and for some later, when you receive the bill. Life is a fair trade; all adjusts itself therein in its own time.

Masters are those who master self;
Teachers are those who teach self;
Governors are those who govern self; and
Rulers are those who rule self.

One who is frightened of the vice is subject to the vice.
One who is addicted to the vice is its captive.
One who acquaints oneself with the vice is the pupil of the vice, and learns a lesson from it.
But one who passeth through the vice and riseth above it is master and conqueror.

The simpleton eats more than they can assimilate.
The simpleton collects more load than they can carry.
The simpleton cuts the same branch of the tree on which they sit.
The simpleton spreads thorns in their own path.

Those who say "I cannot tolerate" show their smallness.
Those who say "I cannot endure" show their weakness.
Those who say "I cannot associate" show their limitation.
Those who say "I cannot forgive" show their imperfection.

Who have failed themselves have failed all; who have conquered themselves have won all.

Happy is one who does good to others; and miserable is one who expects good from others.

Love that is progressive is like the sweet water of the running river, but love that doth not progress is like the salt water of the sea.

It is wicked to pick holes in people;
it is clever to see through subtle ways;
it is foolish to be taken in by people;
it is wise to see all things and overlook them.

One creates one's death; if not so, one was born to live.

Life is a captivity; death is the relief from it.

Belief in God is the fuel, love of God is the glow, and the realization of God is the flame of divine light.

The first birth is the birth of a person; the next birth is the birth of God.

What Brahma creates in a year, Vishnu enjoys for a day, and Shiva destroys in a moment.

Success leads to success, and failure follows a failure.

It is simple to tie a knot of attachment, but it is difficult when you wish to unravel it.

Good praises good; bad fights bad.

The difference between war and peace is that war is using sword against another and peace is using sword toward oneself.

Fight against the enemy means war. Fight against oneself means peace.

Snakes breed under a throne, and scorpions multiply under a crown.

If you are subtle and intelligent, that is natural; but if you are simple and wise, you are a mystery.

We must forget the past, manage the present, and prepare the future.

Mountains can be broken through, the ocean can be crossed, a way may be made through the air, but you cannot find a way to work with those who are hardened in their character, deep-set in their ideas, and fixed in their outlook on life.

What science cannot declare, art can suggest.
What art suggests silently, poetry speaks out.
But what poetry fails to explain in words is expressed by music.

One who does not lose the opportunity of doing some good in life is good;
and one who seizes upon such an opportunity when it occurs is better still;
but one who always looks out for an opportunity to bring some good is best among people.

One who appeals to the human intellect will knock at the gate of the human brain—that one is a speaker.
One who appeals to the human emotions will enter into the hearts of people—that one is a preacher.
But one who penetrates the spirit of his or her hearers is the prophet who will abide in their souls forever.

Passion is the smoke and emotion is the glow of love's fire;
selflessness is the flame that illuminates the path.

Those who have spent have used;
those who have collected have lost;
but those who have given have saved their treasure forever.

One who knows not the truth is a child;
one who is seeking truth is a youth;
but one who has found truth is an old soul.

Be contented with what you possess in life; be thankful for what does not belong to you, for it is so much care the less; but try to obtain what you need in life, and make the best of every moment of your life.

The rock can be cut and polished; hard metal can be melted and molded; but the mind of the foolish person is most difficult to work with.

From the body of love comes reciprocity; from the heart of love comes beneficence; but from the soul of love is born renunciation.

Make your heart as soft as wax to sympathize with others; but make it as hard as a rock to bear the hard knocks of the world.

The path of freedom does not lead to the goal of freedom; it is the path of discipline that leads to the goal of liberty.

The present is the reflection of the past, and the future is the re-echo of the present.

Strength increases strength, and weakness brings a greater weakness.

Translation is a reincarnation, and interpretation is transmigration of an idea.

One's worry is in vain who thinks why others are not what they ought to be; but one who asks why one is not what one ought to be is wise.

A person who fights their nature for their ideal is a saint; a person who subjects their ideal to their realization of truth is the master.

To an angelic soul love means glorification; to a jinn soul love means admiration; to a human soul love means affection; to an animal soul love means passion.

One is living whose sympathy is awake, and one is dead whose heart is asleep.

What you create blindly your intelligence destroys, and what your wisdom creates is destroyed by your ignorance.

People are their own example; if they be false, all is false to them, and if they be true, all is true to them.

Whichever path you choose to tread, the right or the wrong, there is at the back always a powerful hand to push you along.

Those who can live up to their ideal are the sovereigns of life; and those who cannot live up to it are life's slave.

When one denies what one owes you, then it is put on the account of God.

The unselfish profits by life more than the selfish one, whose profit in the end proves to be a loss.

Among a million believers in God there is scarcely one who makes God a reality.

If you live in the vision of the past, dream on, do not open your eyes to the present.
If you live in the eternal now, go on, do not trouble about the morrow.
But if you live for the time to come, do all you can to prepare the future.

It is better to refuse than to accept anything unwillingly.

There is no end to reproaches in one's life, not only those at a distance and those near to one, but even the members of one's body will some day reproach one for not having received proper care and full attention.

The one who holds the world is vaster than the world, and one whom the world holds is small.

There is as much likeness between falsehood and truth as there is between the person and their shadow, the difference being that while the former has life, the latter has none.

When one rises above the earth, the earth is at one's feet; but when one falls beneath the earth,
the earth is over one's head.

Tanas

Sundew, why is it that every insect that kisses you dies instantly?
I like him so much that I eat him up.

Sundew, where did you learn this moral?
A voice said to me, "I am the love and I am the life, and whoever cometh to me by one embrace I turn him into my own life."

Celandines, what do you signify?
We are the lights of the earth.

Rosebud, what were you doing at night?
I was praying to heaven with closed hands to open my heart.

Waterlily, what do you represent by your white garland?
The purity of the heart of this lake.

Tulip, why have you opened your lips?
To tell you what I have learnt in silence.
What did you learn?
To make of oneself an empty cup.

Orchid, what do your petals represent?
Graceful movements of dance.
What does your dance express?
The earth paying homage to heaven.

Little daisies, why do you keep so close to the earth?
Because earth is the home of all mortal beings.

Little daisies, what gospel do you read?
Blessed are the meek, for they shall inherit the earth.

Little daisies, what are you here for?
To represent heaven on earth.

Little daisies, what are you doing here in the churchyard?
We worship God by bowing at the feet of God's creatures.

Cactus, why are you fringed with thorns?
I am the tongue of the malicious person.

Cactus, why is your stem so thorny?
I am the hand of the evildoer.

Cactus, why have you thorns on your leaf?
I am the heart of the wicked who take pleasure in hurting others.

Beautiful gorses, what are you?
We are little lanterns on your path.
But where do you get your prickly thorns?
Flowers from above and thorns from below.

Rosebush, what are you? Friend or foe?
I am both. I have my flowers and thorns.

Wheat grains, why do you grow so close together?
Unity is our strength; that is why you seek in us your life's subsistence.

Palm tree, what do your outstretched hands signify?
I raise hands heavenward when I pray, then pass the blessing on to the earth.

Fir trees, what are you?
We are the souls of the sages who preferred vigil in the solitude to the busy life of the world.

Fir trees, what are you?
We are hands from heaven, stretched out to bless the earth continually.

Fir trees, what are you made for?
We are the temples made for those who worship God in nature.

Fir trees, what are you doing in this forest?
We are the souls on the cross, patiently awaiting the hour of our liberation.

Dry wood, why do they burn you?
Because I no longer can bear fruit.

Thunderstorm, what arouses your passion?
The beauty of the earth.

Full moon, where will you be going from here?
Into retreat.
Why do you take a retreat after your fullness?
To make myself an empty cup in order to rise again.

Church bell, what do you call out?
Every head that resounds like me, it spreads abroad the Message of God.

Church bell, what do you repeat?
The Sacred Name of God, which resounds through my whole being.

Church bell, what makes you move?
The Word of God.

Incense, what do you teach at the church?
One who endureth pain for the cause of others must rise from the mortal world to the spheres of immortality.

Incense, what were you whispering at the church service?
No prayer can reach God unless it arises from a glowing heart.

Incense, what does your scent signify?
My scent is the evidence of my self-sacrifice.

Incense, tell me the secret of your self.
I am the feeling heart of the lover whose deep sigh rises upward, spreading its perfume all around.

Incense, tell me what moral is veiled in your nature?
When my heart endures the test of fire, my hidden quality becomes manifest.

Coin, what are you?
I am the seal of hearts. A heart once sealed by me will love no one but me.

Money, when you leave, what becomes of your lover?
I leave behind a mark on my lover's heart, which always remains as a wound.

Money, what do you like the most?
Changing hands.

Money, which is your dwelling place?
The heart of my worshipper.

Money, where do you accumulate?
Where I am warmly welcomed.

Money, where do you stay?
Where I am worshipped.

Money, whom do you seek?
Who seeks after me.

Money, whom do you worship?
Who has risen above me; I become their slave and live as dust at their feet.

Devil, where do you find your location?
In doubting eyes, in a sharp tongue, in a gossiping mouth, in inquisitive ears, in idle hands, in restless feet, in a vicious body, in a crooked mind, in a bitter heart, and in a darkened soul.

Devil, how do you worship yourself?
In winking eyes, in sneering smiles, in cutting words, and in false tears.

There is one thing that has no answer, and that is, "Why?"
Why? I have no answer for you.
Why? The proper answer for you is, "Why?"
Why? You are yourself the cover over the answer you want.
Why? What a pity you are blind.

Why, what are you?
I am the cry of the hungry mind.

Why, what do you signify?
I am the knocker upon the closed door to which I am attached.

Why, what do you represent?
The owl who cannot see during the day.

Why, what is your complaint?
I am the irritation of mind.

Why, what is your life's condition?
I am shut up in a dark room.

Why, how long will your captivity last?
All night long.

Why, what are you so eagerly waiting for?
The daybreak.

Matchstick, what did you say when I struck you?
Why?

My moods, what are you?
We are the waves rising in your heart.

Emotion, where do you come from?
From the ever-running spring of the heart.

Imagination, what are you?
I am the fountain stream that rises from the mind.

VADAN

The Divine Symphony

Alapa: A divine word in the form of advice.

Alankara: The fanciful expression of an idea.

Bola: A great idea in a few burning words.

Chala: A definite statement.

Gamaka: What comes from the heart of the poet, resisting the attempt to keep it back, keyed to various notes.

Gayatri: Sacred chant.

Raga: The outpouring of the soul.

Sura: God speaking through the kindled soul.

Tala: A rhythm formed by comparison.

Tana: The soul speaking with nature.

Alapas

Is love pleasure, is love merriment? No, love is longing constantly; love is persevering unweariedly; love is hoping patiently; love is willing surrender; love is regarding constantly the pleasure and displeasure of the beloved, for love is resignation to the will of the possessor of one's heart; it is love that teaches one: Thou, not I.

Love that ends is the shadow of love; true love is without beginning or end.

When God gives a blow, God may give you a blow even by the hand of your most loving friend; and when God caresses, God may caress you by the hand of your bitterest enemy.

Let courage be thy sword and patience be thy shield.

Wide space, the womb of my heart, conceive my thought, I pray, and give birth to my desire.

Every soul's seeking I am,
Every heart listens to my call,
Everybody is working for me,
My friend and my foe, one and all.

My thoughts I have sown on the soil of your mind,
My word I have put in your mouth,
My work is given in your hand,
My love radiates in your heart,
My light has illuminated your whole being.

We have made all forms in order to complete the image of the human being.

One day I met the Sovereign face-to-face, and, bending my knees, I prayed, "Tell me, O Sovereign of Compassion, is it Thou who punishest the sinner and givest rewards to the virtuous one?" "No," said Sovereign, smiling, "the sinners attract their punishment; the virtuous earn their reward."

Alankaras

No claim, however big, can be equal to what you are, my mysterious self; and yet you cannot prove the least worthy of the smallest profession you may make.

Unveil Thy face, O God, that I may behold Thy vision.

Expand my heart, God, to the width of the sky, that the whole cosmos be reflected in my soul.

Wherever Thou shalt cast thy glance, Beloved, a new sun will rise there.

Lift my soul, air, and carry it to God's divine spheres.

Let my heart reflect Thy light, O God, as in a pool of water the sun is reflected.

When I see Thy glorious vision, I am moved to ecstasy, Beloved: waves rise in my heart, and my heart turns into the sea.

In the form of flowers I behold Thy image.

Thy invasion as through the storm arouses my deepest passion for Thee.

O nature sublime, speak to me through silence, for I am awaiting in silence, like you, the call of God.

Light is Thy face, and shade is Thy bosom, O Beloved.

Love, I don't know whether to call thee my enemy or friend.
Thou raisest me to the highest heaven, and thou throwest me deep into the infernal regions.
Thou leadest me astray, and it's thou alone who guidest me on the right path.
From thee, O Love, all virtues I draw, and thou art the source of all my sins.
Love, thou art a curse and bliss at the same time.

Empower my heart that I may pull myself together like the heart of the rose controlling its petals.

Beloved, the casting of Thy glance causeth the sun to rise, and when Thy head is turned, the sun sets.

The air brings Thy Message and turns me into ecstasy.

I have loved in life, and I have been loved.
I have drunk the bowl of poison from the hands of Love as nectar and have been raised above
life's joy and sorrow.
My heart, aflame in love, set afire every heart that came in touch with it.
My heart hath been rent and joined again,
My heart hath been broken and again made whole,
My heart hath been wounded and healed again;
A thousand deaths my heart hath died, and thanks be to Love, it liveth yet.
I went through hell and saw there Love's raging fire, and I entered heaven

illumined with the light of Love.
I wept in love and made all weep with me,
I mourned in love and pierced the hearts of men,
And when my fiery glance fell on the rocks, the rocks burst
forth as volcanoes.
The whole world sank in the flood caused by my one tear,
With my deep sigh the earth trembled, and when I cried aloud
the name of my beloved
I shook the throne of God in heaven.
I bowed my head low in humility, and on my knees I begged of
Love,
"Disclose to me, I pray thee, O Love, thy secret."
She took me gently by my arms and lifted me above the earth,
and spoke softly in my ear:
"My dear one, thou thyself art love, art lover, and thyself art the
beloved whom thou hast adored."

Let the heavens be reflected in the earth, my Liege, that the earth may turn into heaven.

Let Thy Word, God, become my life's expression.

Talk through me, my God, the ears of my heart are listening.

My holy pilgrimage is the sacred dwelling of the sage.

It is Thou who comest on earth to save humanity in the form of the sage.

Teach me, O God, through the words of Thy Messenger.

Thou knowest all my needs, and Thou shalt grant them.
O Knower of my heart, fulfill my desires.

O Love, I would be a slave at thy mercy rather than a king free of thee.

Let me forget myself in Thy consciousness.

Nature softly whispers Thy Word to my ears.

In Thy nature I feel Thy presence, O Creator, who art hidden under Thy wonderful creation.

Let Thy might be my might to lift the mountains of life's responsibility.

In the human I see, my beloved God, Thine own image.

I stand at Thy gate when I am in the presence of humankind.

I find Thy shrine at the human heart.

Thy divine mercy is reflected through the heart of the mother.

Speak, God, to me through Thy nature.

My soul's ideal is manifest to me in the human form.

In human arms I experience Thy divine embrace.

My feeling heart is drawn to Thee, dear God, when Thou comest in human form.

I see Thy divine purity in the innocent face of the child.

Whenever I nod to anyone, I bow before Thy throne.

In showing my sympathy to anyone I express my love to Thee, my Beloved.

Teach me innocence, O God, through the child, an angel on earth.

I stand as a bridge between Thee and Thy nature.

My heart stands in waiting and hope as the trees stand still through the darkness of night.

Wide horizon, thou makest my heart wide as thyself.

Thou art the life and Thou art life's sustenance.

My lips are closed, with prayer in them, as the rosebud.

Riding on the horse of hope,
Holding in my hand the rein of courage,
Clad in the armor of patience,
And the helmet of endurance on my head,
I started on my journey to the land of love.

A lance of stern faith in my hand,
And the sword of firm conviction buckled on,
With the knapsack of sincerity
And the shield of earnestness,
I advanced on the path of love.

My ears closed to the disturbing noise of the world,
My eyes turned from all that was calling me on the way,
My heart beating the rhythm of my ever-rising aspiration,
And my blazing soul guiding me on the path,
I made my way through the space.

I went through the thick forests of perpetual desire,
I crossed the running rivers of longing.
I passed through the deserts of silent suffering,
I climbed the steep hills of continual strife.

Feeling ever some presence in the air,
I asked, "Are you there, my love?"
And a voice came to my ears, saying,
"No, still further am I."

Sublime nature, thy reflection produces in my heart God's glorious vision.

I bend toward the Mother Earth in delight of the Father in heaven.

Flowers are Thy dancing rhythm.

I look up to Thee with raised head and hands stretched in worship as the mountains.

Let me greet You in space, O formless and colorless God.

When I am absorbed in Thy glorious vision, Beloved, even my teardrops turn into stars.

Open a way through Thy heavens, that I may arrive at Thy dwelling place.

Let my soul reflect Thy light, that every glance I cast may become a comet.

The divine spark in me is as a drop from Thy ocean; let me preserve it as the rose preserves the dewdrop.

Let the sun of Thy glory shine in my heart.

Let me unite with Thee at the sunset.

Lift, God, the curtain, which divides Thee from me.

Guide me aright, my Liege, I am as a child in Thy divine path.

In the rose I see Thy delightful countenance.

Let me stand by Truth in all calamities, as the mountain stands unshaken through storms.

I behold through space Thy limitless presence.

Since Thy joyful smile has created a new sun in my heart, I see the sun shine everywhere.

Let my soul advance toward Thee, as the rising moon progresses toward fullness.

Silent voice, in the stillness of night I hear thy whisper.

The gently blowing wind kindles the fire of my heart.

When I see in Thy hand an unsheathed sword, Beloved, blood gushes out of my heart as the rising spring.

Send the shower of Thy mercy and compassion on humanity.

Let my heart melt in Thy light as the snow before the sun.

Every leaf becomes Thy finger when Thou fillest the flute with Thy breath.

My soul is still pointing to Thee, though my life is going through a storm.

Providence, allow me to hold long life's glorious moments, I pray, for the time that is once past will never return.

Thou art patiently awaiting the moment to manifest through the silence of sublime nature.

In the light I see Thy beauty, in shade I find Thy mystery.

Let Thy servant, O Liege, be my master.

Though the ever-moving life is my nature, thou art my very being, O stillness.

All light is Thy radiance, and shade is the shadow of Thy beauty.

My soul blows toward Thee as the wind.

Let Thy knowledge cover my heart as the snow covers the ground.

The sweet fragrance of the flowers brings to me the message of Thy sweetness.

My heart has become an ocean, Beloved, since thou hast poured thy love into it.

I see Thy hand blessing me.

Earth into earth, water into water, let my soul immerse into Thee through space.

I hear thy whisper, Beloved, in the morning breeze.

Open my heart that Thy stream may rise up as the spring.

My soul is Thy spirit, O Rasul, now I exist no more.

It is Thou whom I see in all the names and forms.

Thou art closer to me than myself.

Let Thy might strengthen me, Thy light inspire me, and let Thy love move my soul to the ultimate joy.

My life is running toward Thee, my ocean, as the river runs to the sea.

In the color of flowers I see the color of Thy countenance.

Make me conscious of Thee, that I may lose the consciousness of my being.

Let every movement of life whisper Thy Name to my ears.

Thou blowest my heart's fire by fanning it with the fluttering leaves.

Light is Thine eye, Beloved, and shade is its pupil.

God, be Thou before me when I am awake and within me when I am asleep.

In my veneration for the aged I worship Thee, O God.

I drink the wine of Thy presence and lose myself in its intoxication.

Let my spirit reflect, O Beloved, the beauty of Thy color and form.

Let my heart bloom in Thy love as the rose.

As invisible as space and as inconceivable as time is Thy being, O God!

Teach me, God, to walk over life's sea.

Let me receive Thy Message as the branches that swing in ecstasy.

O sublime nature, in thy stillness let my heart rest.

In the light Thou are manifest, in the shade Thou art hidden.

One more cup, my Beloved, that I may entirely lose myself.

I see the Beloved's beauty in all colors and forms.

The flowers tell me how beautiful Thou art.

Fill my heart with Thy beauty as Thou fillest empty space with Thy creation.

Light represents Thy heavens and shade Thy earth.

Gentle breeze, thy touch to me is the caress of the Beloved.

Raise my soul toward Thee with the rise of the sun.

The sun sets,
The moon wanes,
The spring passes,
The year ends.
I asked of life: "Tell me,
how long will you continue to be?"
"I," said life, "I will live forever."

Air, carry the Message of my feeling heart, far and beyond.

We shall see who will endure to the end, my persevering adversary or my patience.

The waves of the sea, even as I, rise with outstretched hands to reach Thee, God, and fall at thy feet in ecstasy.

O nature sublime, pregnant with divine spirit, thou speakest the prayer that riseth from my heart.

Let my heart reflect Thy divine light as the moon reflects the sun.

Happiness, certainly thou didst play hide-and-seek with me since I have been in thy pursuit. I saw in the world thy shadow cast, and in paradise I saw thy reflection. In pleasure I saw a veil over thy beautiful face, in pain I saw the dust lying humbly under thy feet.

My intuition, hast thou ever deceived me? No, never; it is my reason that so often deludeth me, for it cometh from without. Thou art rooted within my heart.

Let me be melted in Thy divine ocean as a pearl in wine.

Alone on the sea, alone on land, in the crowd, in solitude, alone I stand.

My considerate self, seek not pleasure through the pain of another, life through the death of another, gain through the loss of another, and honor through the humiliation of another.

Let my life become the spring of Thy infinite life, running eternally forever and ever.

I see Thy mystery hidden under the petals of the flowers.

My heart, hold closely that oil that keeps the light burning.

Pain, my lifelong comrade, if all went and left me, you would still be there.

With the opening and closing of Thine eyes, Beloved, the sun rises and sets in my heart.

My self, how nice it is to feel that if no one in the world understood me, still you would understand.

The air moves my heart to tears in Thy love.

Those who are given liberty to act freely by God are nailed on the earth, and those who are free to act as they choose on the earth will be nailed in the heavens.

My sense of shame, did I not suffer in feeding thy vanity?

Out of flowers comes a fragrance, which moves my heart to ecstasy.

Let me not be drowned in the sea of mortal life.

Speak, God, in silence; this moment my heart is in tune with the stillness of Thy nature.

My endurance, thou hast crushed me until I became thy clay kneaded to make a body for the Divine Spirit.

O nature sublime, in Thy silence I hear Thy cry.

Ever-moving sea of life, am I not but a wave rising in thy heart?

Thanks to the winner of my heart, there is nothing of me left any more.

My thoughtful self,
Bear all and do nothing,
Hear all and say nothing,
Give all and take nothing,
Serve all and be nothing.

While I was roaming through the forest, a thorn pricked my bare foot and cried, "Ah, you have crushed me." I felt sorry and I asked its forgiveness.

A wasp flying in the air stung my arm and cried, "Ah, you have caught me in your sleeve." I felt sorry and I asked its forgiveness.

My foot slipped and I fell in a pool of muddy water. The water cried, "Ah, you have disturbed me." I felt sorry and I asked its forgiveness.

I absently happened to touch a burning fire, and the fire cried, "Ah, you have extinguished me." I felt sorry and I asked its forgiveness.

I asked my gentle self, "Have you received any harm?" "Be thankful," said she, "that is was not worse."

I will soar higher than the highest heaven,
I will dive deeper than the depths of the ocean,
I will reach further than the wide horizon,
I will enter within my innermost being.
You know me but little, O ever-changing life,
I will live in that sphere where death cannot reach.

I will raise my head high before you will turn your back to me,
I will close my lips before you will close the doors of your heart,
I will dry my tears before you will not respond to my sigh,
I will fly to the heavens, O world of illusion, before you will
throw me down on the earth.

Golden Rules

My conscientious self:
Keep to your principles in prosperity as well as in adversity.
Be firm in faith through life's tests and trials.
Guard the secrets of friends as your most sacred trust.
Observe constancy in love.
Break not your word of honor whatever may befall.
Meet the world with smiles in all conditions of life.
When you possess something, think of the one who does not possess it.
Uphold your honor at any cost.
Hold your ideal high in all circumstances.
Do not neglect those who depend upon you.

Silver Rules

My conscientious self:
Consider duty as sacred as religion.
Use tact on all occasions.
Place people rightly in your estimation.
Be no more to anyone than you are expected to be.
Have regard for the feelings of every soul.
Do not challenge anyone who is not your equal.
Do not make a show of your generosity.
Do not ask a favor of those who will not grant it you.
Meet your shortcomings with a sword of self-respect.
Let not your spirit be humbled in adversity.

Copper Rules

My conscientious self:
Consider your responsibility sacred.
Be polite to all.
Do nothing which will make your conscience feel guilty.
Extend your help willingly to those in need.
Do not look down upon the one who looks up to you.
Judge not another by your own law.
Bear no malice against your worst enemy.
Influence no one to do wrong.
Be prejudiced against no one.
Prove trustworthy in all your dealings.

Iron Rules

My conscientious self:
Make no false claims.
Speak not against others in their absence.
Do not take advantage of a person's ignorance.
Do not boast of your good deeds.
Do not claim that which belongs to another.
Do not reproach others, making them firm in their faults.
Do not spare yourself in the work which you must accomplish.
Render your services faithfully to all who require them.
Seek not profit by putting someone in straits.
Harm no one for your own benefit.

Suras

Verily, the domain of every soul is in its own sphere.

Verily, the one in whose heart my star shineth is blessed.

Verily, the one who liveth religion through life in the world is really pious.

Verily, every action sets in movement each atom of the universe.

Verily, in the human is reflected all that is on earth and in heaven.

Verily, the power of the word can move mountains.

Verily, the one who knows the influence of time knows the secret of life.

Verily, a person is a mind.

Verily, spirit hath all the power there is.

When God gives, God generously gives, even through the hand of your worst enemy; and when God is determined to take, God takes away even by the hand of your best friend.

Death takes away the weariness of life, and the soul begins life anew.

Death is a sleep from which one wakes up in the hereafter.

Death is the crucifixion after which follows the resurrection.

After the night of death is passed, the day of life begins.

Life never dies, it is death which is dead. It is death which dies, not life.

The everlasting life is hidden in the heart of death.

Ragas

Beloved, Thou makest me fuller every day.
Thou diggest into my heart deeper than the depths of the earth.
Thou raisest my soul higher than the seventh heaven,
    making me more empty every day and yet fuller.
Thou makest me larger than the ends of the world.
Thou stretchest my two arms across the land and sea,
    giving into my enfoldment the East and the West.
Thou changest my flesh into fertile soil.
Thou turnest my blood into streams of water.
Thou kneadest my clay, I know, to make a new universe.

In the swinging of the branches, in the flying of the birds, and in the running of the water, Beloved, I see Thy waving hand bidding me goodbye.

In the cooing of the wind, in the roaring of the sea, and in the crashing of the thunder, Beloved, I see Thee weep and I hear Thy cry.

In the promise of the dawn, in the breaking of the morn, in the smiles of the rose, Beloved, I feel Thy joy at my homecoming.

Let Thy wish become my desire,
Let Thy will become my deed.
Let Thy word become my speech, my Beloved, and
Let Thy love become my creed.

Let my plant bring forth Thy flowers,
Let my fruits produce Thy seed,
Let my heart become Thy lute, Beloved,
And my body Thy flute of reed.

When I close my eyes in the solitude, I see Thy glorious vision
    in my heart;
And, opening my eyes amidst the crowd, I see Thee acting on
    the stage of this earth.
Always I am in Thy dazzling presence, my Beloved;
Thou takest me to heaven and Thou bringest me on earth in the
    twinkling of an eye.

Let me not fall low after having raised me high; let me not become narrow after having made me broad. Let me not become small after having once made me great; throw me not down, Beloved, after once Thou hast lifted me up.

I looked and looked to find someone to whom I could give my trust, but I saw no one until I found Thee, O Thou who art hidden in my heart, holding in Thy hand the record of my life's secret.

As I put myself forward into the world so I show my limitation, my Sovereign; but as I withdraw myself from the world so I enter into Thy kingdom.

I look to Thee, O Sovereign, when the noose of death
seems unavoidable and nigh.
I look to Thee, O Sovereign, when with heavy heart
I see my beloved ones depart.
I look to Thee, O Sovereign, when limit and change
in the worldly love I see.
I look to Thee, O Sovereign, when all that I call mine
is snatched away from my hand.
I look to Thee, O Sovereign, when my boon companions
of joy turn their back in my sorrow.
I look to Thee, O Sovereign, when my hands are full
with worldly strife.
I look to Thee, O Sovereign, when the higher self raises me up
and my lower self weighs me down.
I look to Thee, O Sovereign, when I try to do right
and it turns to wrong.
I look to Thee, O Sovereign, when all in life seems as naught
to me,
and a seeking I feel for something beyond.

The spring that riseth out of Thy heart, Thou pourest upon me, and my spirit feels the exaltation of being dissolved under Thy divine shower.

When Thou didst sit upon Thy throne with a crown upon Thy
head, I did prostrate myself upon the ground and called
Thee my Sovereign.
When Thou didst stretch out Thy hands in blessing over me,
I knelt and called Thee my Liege.
When Thou didst raise me from the ground, holding me with
Thine arms, I drew closer to Thee and called Thee my
Beloved.
But when Thy caressing hands held my head next to Thy

glowing heart and Thou didst kiss me, I smiled and called Thee myself.

What I may not see, let me not see.
What I may not hear, let me not hear.
What I may not know I ask not to know.
Beloved, I am contented with both Thy speech and Thy silence.

Let those not see me who should not see me.
Let those not hear me who will not hear me.
Let those not know me who need not know me.
Beloved, veil me and unveil me as Thy wisdom chooseth.

I see Thy skill, O perfect Artist, in the making of flowers.
Who made the flowers so beautiful, colored them, and gave them fragrance? It is Thee, my Sovereign.

Let my insight be deeper than the ocean; let my mind be more fertile than the land; let my heart be wider than the horizon, Beloved; and let my soul soar higher than Paradise.

Every form I see is Thine own form, my Sovereign.
Every sound I hear is Thine own voice.
In the fragrance I smell the perfume of Thy Spirit.
In every word spoken to me, I hear Thy voice, my Sovereign.
All that touches me is Thine own touch.
In everything I taste I experience the syrup of Thy delicious Spirit.
In every place I recognize Thee, my Sovereign.
Every word that touches my ears is Thy Message.
Everything that touches me thrills me with the joy of Thy kiss.
Wherever I roam I need Thee, wherever I reach I find Thee, my Sovereign.

Wherever I look I see Thy glorying face, whatever I touch, I
touch Thy beloved hand.
Whomever I see, I see Thee in their soul.
From whomever I take anything, I take it from Thee.
To whomever I give something, I give it humbly to Thee.
Whoever cometh to me, to me it is Thy call.
On whomever I call, I call at Thy own gate.

Turn me not aside, Beloved, once Thou hast granted me Thy favor.
Starve me not of a kiss, after Thou hast enfolded me.
Grieve me not, Beloved, since Thou hast made me smile.
Turn not away Thine eyes, once Thou hast poured the wine of
Thy magic glance into the cup of my heart.

Enter unhesitatingly, Beloved, for in this abode there is naught
but my longing for Thee.

Do I call Thee my soul? But Thou art my spirit.
Can I call Thee my life? But Thou livest forever.
May I call Thee my Beloved? But Thou art Love itself.
Then what must I call Thee? I must call Thee myself.

Why did I not recognize Thee when first I opened my eyes on
the earth?
Why did I not respond to Thee when I heard Thy enchanting
voice?
Why did I not feel Thy gentle hand when Thou didst caress my
face?
Why did I not cling to Thee, Beloved, when Thou lovingly didst
kiss my lips?
When I began to look for Thee, in the twinkling of an eye Thou
didst disappear.

When I started in Thy pursuit, Thou didst move away from me
still farther.
When I called Thee aloud in my distress, Thou didst not hear
my soul's bitter cry.
Cross-legged I sat in silence; then alone I heard Thy call.

Why have I two eyes if not to behold Thy glorious vision?
Why have I two ears if not to hear Thy gentle whisper?
Why have I the sense of smell if not to breathe the essence of
Thy spirit?
Why have I two lips, Beloved, if not to kiss Thy beautiful
countenance?
Why have I two hands if not to work in Thy divine cause?
Why have I two legs if not to walk in Thy spiritual path?
Why have I a voice if not to sing Thy celestial song?
Why have I a heart, Beloved, if not to make it Thy sacred
dwelling?

Did I not leave the unseen world in Thy pursuit?
Have I not come to this world of limitations in search of Thee?
Have I not followed Thy footprints on this earth?
Have I not looked for Thy light in the heavens?
But where did I find Thee, Beloved, at last?
Hiding in my heart.

Every step in Thy path draws me nearer to Thee, every breath in Thy thought exhilarates my spirit, every glimpse of Thy smile is inspiring to my soul, every tear in Thy love, Beloved, exalts my being.

Tanas

Little dandelions, what are you doing here?
We are the reflection on earth of the stars in heaven.

Little pool, why is your water muddy?
Because of my narrow mind and depthless heart.

Coal, what does your blackness signify?
I am the evil accumulated in the heart of the earth.

What is your destiny?
I must pass through a trial by fire.

Earth to the clouds: Why did you come back after once you had deserted me?
The heavens would not have us before we had reconciled ourselves with you.

Beautiful rosebud, what do you hold between your hands?
The secret of my beauty.

Sunflower, what are you?
I am the eye of the seeker whose search is after light.

Death, what are you?
I am the shadow of life.

Death, what are you born of?
I am born of ignorance.

Death, where is your abode?
My abode is in the mind of the illusion.

Death, do you ever die?
Yes, when pierced by the arrow of the seer's glance.

Death, whom do you draw near to you?
I draw closer those who are attracted to me.

Death, whom do you love?
I love those who long for me.

Death, whom do you attend?
I readily attend to those who call on me.

Death, whom do you scare?
I frighten the one who is not familiar with me.

Death, whom do you caress?
The one who lies trustfully in my arms.

Death, with whom are you severe?
I am hard on those who do not readily respond to my call.

Death, whom do you serve?
I serve the godly; when they return home I carry their baggage.

Boat:
I take you in my bosom on the water.

Wagon:
I carry you on my back on the land.

Rose flower, why are your lips drooping down?
I am thinking over my glorious past.

Rose flower, what are you saying with your lips open?
I am speaking of my glorious past.

Why do you rise, waves, with the coming of the wind?
To receive the Message it brings.

Moth to the flame: What have you done?
I gave you my life, what have you done for me?

Flame:
I allowed you to kiss me.

Sea, why is your color blue?
It is heaven reflected in my white heart.

Earth, tell me of your moral principle?
Those who pass over me, I lay my self before them; and those who come unto me, I open to them my heart.

Wind, what makes the sea respond to you so wholeheartedly?
In her I have touched her deepest chord.

Wind, what spell did you cast upon the sea to move its whole being to passion?
Nothing, only a kiss.

"So" gives rise to an argument, "Why?" continues it, and it ends in "No."

What sense is there, O moth, in burning yourself by trying to kiss the light?
My joy in it is greater than my sacrifice.

Waves, why does wind come and then go from you?
It comes to wake us and leaves us to solve the problem among ourselves.

Moving waves, the wind has left you and you are still in commotion.
We are still repeating the word it has taught us; it moves our whole being to ecstasy.

Waves, why do you all get excited at the same time and become calm together?
Because behind our individual action there is one impulse working.

Rising waves what motive is behind your impulse?
Reaching upward.

Sea, what is it that makes you so chaotic?
No sooner the air whispers to my ears wisdom's message, than an enormous struggle begins within my self.

Storm, you invade us suddenly without any warning.
I sent my ultimatum by the hands of the wind before I started gunfire.

Storm, why are the clouds being scattered?
I have given orders for demobilization.

Storm, why do you send the rain after you have gone?
To make peace with the earth.

Human: "Devil, will you be my friend?"
Devil: "I am at your disposal."

Waves: "Do we not lay ourselves in complete surrender before you for you to pass over us? Then listen to our request:

throw into the water those you carry in your bosom."

Boat: "No, I am not like you who drown beneath your feet those who seek refuge in your arms. The ones whom I hold in my heart, either I sink with them or I carry them safely to their destination."

"Earthly riches, explain to me your character."
"I fly from the hand that holds me, I escape from the one who pursues me, I fall into the purse of the one who collects me, I live with the one who spares me, I leave the one who does not look after me, I keep away from the one who has me not. The one who does not possess me is poor indeed, but the one who possesses me is poorer still."

Gamakas

I would rather have a lasting pain than a pleasure that passes away.

My mind never changes, but I change my mind whenever I wish.

My soul often has the feeling of being stretched, held fast by the heavens and pulled continually by the earth.

My errors do not lull me to sleep, but they open my eyes to a deeper vision of life.

My smallest work in the inner plane is worth more than all I do in the outer world.

No sooner is my heart struck than a switch is turned and the light appears.

All that I can manage in life, I take as my responsibility, but all that I cannot manage, I leave to God.

When I try to do some good to others, I never think it is enough; but when I receive the slightest good from others, I feel it is more than sufficient.

When I open my eyes to the outer world, I feel myself as a drop in the sea; but when I close my eyes and look within, I see the whole universe as a bubble raised in the ocean of my heart.

How did I rise above narrowness?
The edges of my own walls began to hurt me, and I was obliged to rise above them.

I would die proud rather than live a long life of humiliation.

All that has passed I attribute to fate, but I feel myself responsible for all that is to be done.

The Scriptures have called God the Creator, the Masons have termed God the Architect, but I know God as the Actor on this stage of life.

I respect all those of great names, but seek continually after the Nameless.

I am resigned to the past, attentive to the present, and hopeful for the future.

I accept no refusal from the heavens.

Christ—his image in the church, his spirit in my soul.

I have not come to teach you what you know not, I have come to deepen in you that wisdom that is yours already.

One who has lost me is lost; one who has found me has found life eternal.

My presence stimulates in your heart that feeling that must always be kept alive.

Be not disappointed if I tell you things that are already known to you. Know that they can never be repeated too many times.

There is nothing too good or too bad for me since I am conscious of that reality which is hidden and yet covers all.

I am what I am; by trying to be something I make that self limited who in reality is all.

I do not give you my ideas, what I give you is my personal knowledge.

My heart is the key to the hearts of everyone.

None I need remove to place another in my heart; my heart is large enough to accommodate each and all.

I learn from my murids more than they learn from me.

Neither do I defend the wrongdoers nor do I condemn them.

I try to do right which seems to me right at the moment; at another moment the same thing may seem to me wrong. Therefore I do not attempt to prove my doing right to the one who does not see the right of it.

Nothing new I say when I speak; I only renew the memory of things that may not be forgotten

I play my melody while everyone sings their own song.

My friends lull me to sleep, but my enemies keep me awake.

Praise fans the glow of my heart and blame turns it into a blaze.

What has happened has happened; what I am going through I shall rise above; and what will come I will meet with courage.

While I am working I learn something;
while I am thinking I discern something;
while I am speaking I teach something;
while I am silent I reach something.

Art is dear to my heart, but nature is near to my soul.

If I were not as I am, I would not have been what I am.

When I open my eyes and look at the wide world, I become great;
when I close my eyes and look within, I become greater still.

Bolas

A virtue carried too far may become a sin.

At the very end of the valley of sin you will find virtue.

In the meeting of a glance there is a union of souls.

Success spoils people, failure ruins them.

Things are as you look at them.

One who is never alone does not know the joy of being alone.

The heart that is not struck by the sweet smiles of an infant is still sleeping.

Conception is belief, but conviction is faith.

To love is a sin, and not to love is a crime.

When facts fall dead, truth comes to life.

Nothing matters really, though everything matters.

Neither fight nor embrace evil, simply rise above it.

The pursuit after truth is more interesting than its attainment.

When human love has ceased, divine love springs out.

Smash your ideals against the rock of Truth.

Let your virtues dissolve into the sea of purity.

Make your doctrines fuel for the fire of the intelligence.

You need not trust whom you do not know, as long as you don't distrust them.

It is easy to be just, but difficult to be wise.

If you will not rise above the things of this world, they will rise above you.

Even the wisest person must sometimes stray from wisdom.

Too much enthusiasm pushes the object of attainment farther off.

Anxiety paralyzes activity.

Worry consumes the spirit of action.

Even with God one can find fault, but where is the fault? In the person who finds it.

The load of responsibility weighs upon a soul more than the strain of work.

Perfection forgives, and limitation judges.

A home is made, and a house is built.

Do not let your heart offer anyone such food as will increase their appetite and decrease your fund of supply.

Make the snake your friend rather than your enemy.

All people are equal in truth but not in fact.

What does limit God? God's name.

Life is too small a price to offer to someone whom you really love.

The real learning is unlearning all that one has learned.

To judge people God borrows from them their sense of justice.

To investigate the wrongdoing of someone is like digging deep into the mud.

Prayer is a deep-felt need of the soul.

A person sees the right side of their own mind and the wrong side of another's.

What enables a person to earn a good name? Shame.

Put your theories in practice before you expound them.

First believe in the God Who is all-exclusive, and then realize the God Who is all-inclusive.

As pleasure is the shadow of happiness, so fact is the shadow of truth.

Fact is to be observed in action, and truth in realization.

Usually in everything one says and does one denies reality

Fact is a covering over truth.

Fact or no fact, truth proves and disproves all.

Jealousy is the refuse of the heart.

Pity the wicked ones for their evildoing, for they can do no better.

If there is any place where one can meet with God, it is this earth plane.

Righteousness is nothing but a natural outcome of right thinking.

Every action that defeats its own object is wrong.

No creature in the world is as attractive and as repellent as a human.

Simplicity is the living beauty.

If you do not want to understand, you will not understand.

The one who will not take in the idea of unity, will be taken in by unity someday.

There is no use arguing if you have done wrong or I have done wrong, for all that need be done is to right the wrong.

Life offers opportunity either to pick up pearls and throw away pebbles, or to pick up pebbles and throw away pearls.

Mystics retain something of childhood all through their life.

The realization of truth is the greatest luxury.

Fact is the illusion of truth.

Shadow is the shadow of shadow, not of light; the ego is light itself and so it has no shadow.

The false ego is the shadow of the body seen in the sky, not the reflection of the soul.

Heart talks to heart, soul speaks to soul.

Truth is not acquired but is discovered.

Nature regards no conventionality.

You cannot be too wise, but you can be too clever.

A bitter taste lasts only as long it is in the mouth.

Carry as much load as you may be able to carry easily.

If your heart is large enough there is nothing it will not accommodate.

By calling him by his name you will raise Satan from his grave.

We cannot appreciate another's kindness if we think of what good we have done to the other.

There is no greater teacher for the evildoer than evil itself.

Devotion without wisdom is like salt water.

What were the great personalities whose light has shone upon millions of people? Examples.

The claim of Christhood seemed too great for Jesus, therefore it was that he was crucified by the intolerant world.

Thought and feeling often take opposite directions.

Do not enjoy life more than life allows you to enjoy it; if not, your joy will turn into sorrow.

Hierarchy is the Sufis' way, but equality of all people is their truth.

A person may rise above sins, but not above the reproaches of those who witness.

The clever person knows better how to tell a lie, the wise person knows best how to avoid it.

God is God and human is human, yet God is human and human is God.

Peacemaking is much more difficult than war-making.

It is the dead who cause death, the living preserve life.

You cannot live the truth, but you can realize it.

Wrong is wrong from the beginning to the end, and right is right from the first to the last.

Evil brings success to the wicked, and virtue brings success to the righteous.

Faults and merits both serve as steps to those who go up and those who go down.

It more difficult to tame a human than a lion.

Reason not with those who are incapable of understanding your reason.

Politeness in words and politeness in deeds are two different things.

No one may claim perfection, though everyone may strive after it.

You need not do something today because you did it yesterday.

Cupidity must be renounced, not joy.

The fire of hell does not burn the sinners, it only burns their sins.

Wisdom is the way in which to express life as one has understood it oneself.

One learns to follow the will of God by practicing self-denial.

Those who are infallible cannot be superhuman; they may be inhuman.

Apart from evil doings, even evil intentions bring about disastrous results.

The knowledge of plurality begins life, but in the consciousness of unity is life's culmination.

Faith reaches beyond the limit of human comprehension.

It is the optimists who take the initiative; the pessimists follow them.

Morality is a flower that springs out of the plant of individuality.

True piety is sincerity.

Principles are to guide our life, not to restrict it.

Love that is free from attachment is the love of sages.

The right attitude in life is to keep a balance between justice and kindness.

The presence of the godly person for me is the sacred river.

It is better not to do than to do things badly.

To analyze love is to destroy love.

Subtle ideas are best expressed simply.

Every body reincarnates, not every soul.

If you say, "I cannot," you will not; if you will, you can.

Love that endureth not is heart's illusion.

When optimism is exhausted, pessimism springs up.

Coming into the presence of the godly, is like entering into the gate of God.

In the union of two loving hearts is the Unity of God.

The sin of the virtuous is a virtue, the virtue of the sinner is a sin.

The shade adds to the light as zero adds to the figure.

The heart of the Holy One is the gate to God's shrine.

Love has its own law.

Beauty is finished in simplicity.

In the spirit of duty there is the soul of religion.

What is rooted out in the quest of Truth is ignorance.

Balance is the keynote of spiritual attainment.

Beauty is not power but its possessor.

Do not fall in love but rise.

What may give vanity to one, may give shame to another.

Great people have great faults, but their greatness is their greatest fault.

Nothing that your mind can conceive does not exist.

Life teaches one more than all the teachings in the world.

An experience gained as late as the last hour of one's life is still a gain.

Nothing is lost as long as your hope is not lost.

All will help you if you will help yourself.

Surprise is nothing but an expression of one's ignorance.

Leave all that unsaid that by being said creates inharmony.

Many say they tell the truth, but few there are who know the truth.

Mystics do not possess knowledge, for they are knowledge.

Mystics do not observe any law, they themselves are the law.

Great gift and no virtue is like a flower without fragrance.

Pleasures cost more than they are worth.

Patient endurance crowns goodness with beauty.

A bad nature is the worst immorality.

One who is understood is under the one who understands him or her.

Passion is but another form of love.

Recognize mystics not from what they do, but from what they are.

Shameless is lifeless.

By rising above facts we touch reality.

It is our words that hide reality.

Outward things matter little, it is inward realization that counts.

Every failure follows upon a weakness somewhere.

Those who cannot help themselves cannot help others.

The wrong use of every good thing is bad, the right use of every bad thing is good.

Hate brings hate to us, and love brings love.

If you begin from the end, you will finally arrive at the beginning.

Beware lest your remedy become your malady.

Will is not a power but all the power there is.

What is God? God is what is wanting to complete oneself.

It is natural that heavenly reason does not agree with earthly reason.

Reasoning is a ladder; by this ladder one can rise, and from this ladder one may fall.

Reason is a great factor and has all possibility in it of every curse and of every bliss.

Daring is preferred to fearing.

A sparkling soul flashes out through the eyes.

A great person is great with their faults and merits.

Be complete here and perfect there.

A wrong direction may lead to quite the opposite end.

Devotion gives all, asks nothing.

Love knows no limits.

Love keeps back nothing.

If you do not see God in the human, you will not see God anywhere.

You can never be sure of anything in this world of illusion.

If you can no longer love, it proves that you never did love.

The way you choose is the way for you.

Feeling is life and death at the same time.

The eyes are two windows through which the soul looks out.

The benefit of the word "Almighty" is in its realization.

The air of heaven a child brings to me when it comes on earth.

What is made for humans, humans may hold; they must not be held by it.

The bringers of joy have always been the children of sorrow.

One enemy can do more harm than the good that can be done by a hundred friends.

The virtue of duty is in the pleasure of doing it.

Duty done unwillingly is worse than slavery.

Who else but a noble soul would bear all and say nothing.

By going through sorrow we rise above it.

Fools fight wisdom wherever they meet it.

By disliking our dislikes we begin to like all things.

Sympathy robs one of oneself.

It is the one who lacks keen observation who becomes critical.

The critical tendency comes from agitation of mind.

Pursuit after the impossible is the best game there is.

The best way to love is to serve.

Some satisfy their vanity at the cost of their lives.

Fishers of men have their net of sympathy.

Sensation is a shadow of exaltation.

The world's end comes with the breaking of the heart.

Renounce the world before the world renounces you.

The wicked world does not allow one's fine feelings to be cherished.

When a loving heart manifests jealousy it is like sweet milk turning sour.

Love creates beauty by her own hands, to worship.

Wisdom is the cream of intelligence.

All learning becomes pale once divine knowledge begins to shine.

A life of superficiality is lived as not lived.

The spirit of the human is the egg in which God is formed.

The human heart is the womb from which the Lord is born.

Talas

There is one individual hidden behind many individualities, there is one person shining through all personalities.

The loveless is lifeless, the loving is living.

One breathes the air of heaven and another experiences the fire of hell, yet both walk on the same earth.

There are some who walk, there are some who creep, there are some who run, and there are others who fly, and yet they are all human beings.

It is unjust to be rich when others are poor, and it is fatal to be poor when others are rich.

A large person will stretch your mind to the breadth of their own heart, and a small person will narrow it to the size of their own outlook.

There is a right side to every wrong, and there is a wrong side to every right.

The mind is its question, and it is itself its answer.

All the lack that we find in life is the lack of will, and all the blessing that comes to us comes by the power of will.

Belief is a thing, but faith is a being.

Thoughts have words, feelings have a voice; words have form, voice has a soul.

There are hearts, the longer they are together, the more attached they become; and there are hearts, the longer they are together the more apart they grow.

Sound is the life of life; time is the death of death.

To love is one thing and to own is another thing.

The wealth-seeker has no regard for father or brother; the pleasure-seeker considers no honor nor respect; the sorrowful has no comfort nor sleep; the hungry distinguishes not between ripe and unripe.

Do I pass through life? No, it is life that passeth by me.

By loving someone you melt your own heart in the fire of love; by possessing someone you make your heart cold.

Possession is self-assertion; loving is self-abnegation. The possessor must lose, sooner or later, the one he or she possesses; the lover gains in the end, if not the beloved, love itself.

The ones who cover their grief under a smile are sincere; the ones who cover their laughter under grief are hypocrites.

Love that depends on being answered by the beloved is lame; it does not stand on its own feet. Love that tries to possess the beloved is without arms; it can never hold. Love that does not regard the pleasure and displeasure of the beloved is blind. Love that is exacting and self-assertive is dead.

The loving souls are blind to the faults of those they love, and the hater is blind to the merits of those they hate.

Wisdom existed before the wise, life existed before the living, love existed before the lover.

Desert can be changed into sown; the land can be changed into the sea; even hell can be changed into heaven; but the mind that is once fixed cannot be changed.

Words are valuable, but silence is precious.

That which fools can say rudely, the clever cover under a veil; and the wise say the same without saying it.

The day you will feel you don't know, you will begin to know.

What is once given is given; what is once done is done; what is once lost is lost; what is once won is won.

Nothing can bind one to the other except one's own sympathy, and nothing can free one from the other but the cutting of that sympathetic thread.

As eagerly inclined as one is to free oneself from a situation, so readily is one inclined to fall into it.

Nothing is as old as the Truth, and nothing is as new as the Truth.

Make of them big things, if you wish do small things; and make of them small things, if you wish to do big things.

We speak when we understand the language of one another, and we keep silent when we feel one another's heart.

Tone is the voice of life; time is the word of death.

There are many sins, small and great, but to recognize sin is the greatest sin.

To step forward is going forward in the path of friendship, and to step backward is going backward.

Those who retort pay back the one who insults them, but those who take silently stand above every insult.

There are two times in life when the danger of falling awaits one: the time of prosperity and the time of adversity.

All things become wrong when they are not in their right time or proper place.

In order to arrive at spiritual attainment two gulfs must be crossed: the sea of attachment and the ocean of detachment.

There is nothing more subtle or simpler than Truth.

Food is the nourishment of the body;
thought is a refreshment to the mind;
love is the subsistence for the heart;
truth is the sustenance of the soul.

One's ideal shows the height of one's heart;
one's understanding shows the depth of one's heart;
one's perception shows the length of one's heart;
one's sympathy shows the breadth of one's heart;
but the fourth dimension of one's heart is seen from all that it contains within itself.

Wisdom is different from justice: while justice is expressed in fairness, wisdom is shown by tact.

There are two sorts of persons who show childlike simplicity in their lives: the silly one, who shows childish traits, and the wise one, who shows innocence.

There are some who make the dead alive, and there are others who make the living dead.

Two persons are silent on the question of religion, the most foolish and the most wise.

Above law is love, and above love is God.

The power of the word is indeed great, but the power of silence is greater still.

One who speaks much and says little is foolish; one who speaks little and says much is wise.

In the drop, the sea is as small as the drop; in the sea, a drop is as large as the sea.

If it is true, it is as true as false; if it is false, it is as false as true.

One stands above the situation who controls it; one falls beneath the situation who becomes involved in it.

One who looks at life with horror is in the underworld; one who takes life seriously to heart is in the world; the one who smiles at life with a happy smile is above the world.

One is foolishly selfish who is selfish, and one is wisely selfish who appears unselfish.

Before one becomes sharp and the other blunt,
Before one is hot and the other cold,
Before one doubts and the other suspects,

Before one gives up one's confidence and the other their trust,
It is time that they had left one another.
Before one closes one's eyes and the other their ears,
Before one turns one's head and the other their back,
Before one talks and the other talks back,
Before one is in wrath and the other in rage,
It is time that they had left one another.

Friendship, relationship, familiarity, intimacy, all have their limits; if you pass beyond that limit, you certainly break law.

There are those who enjoy taking, and there are those who enjoy giving.

If you can say without saying, you better not say. If you can do without doing, you must not do.

Many live to die, and many die to live.

Even the faults of the meritorious soul become merits, and even the merits of the faulty one turn into faults.

There are two kinds of people: those who are blinded by faith, and those who are blind to faith.

One cannot be real and live in the world of falsehood, and one cannot be false and exist in the world of reality.

Love all, trust none;
forgive all, forget none;
respect all, worship none—
that is the manner of the wise.

The rose brings forth fragrance, color, and beautiful structure; so the soul, with its unfoldment, shows personality, atmosphere, and refined manner.

The sun, air, water, space, and fertile soil are necessary for the rose to bloom; intelligence, inspiration, love, a wide outlook, and guidance are required for the soul to unfold.

Art without beauty, poetry without inspiration, music without feeling, science without reason, philosophy without logic, religion without devotion, mysticism without ecstasy are like a lake without water.

A joke without wit, a speech without meaning, tears without romance, learning without wisdom, position without honor, a heart without love, a head without thought are like space without the air.

A man without manly courage, a woman without womanly grace, a child without a child's simplicity, an infant without an infant's innocence, a lover without willing sacrifice, a worshipper without the ideal of God, a giver without great modesty are like a king without a kingdom.

Criticism, indifference, and pessimism are the three things that close the door of the heart.

Love is the object in the life of both devil and saint. The one demands it, the other gives it.

God created man in his own image, and man made God in his own likeness.

What pleasure is there in a useless action?
What interest is there in a senseless speech?

What joy is there in a depthless thought?
What happiness is there in a loveless feeling?

The image of Christ is in the Church, the book of Christ is with the clergy, the love of Christ is in the heart of his worshipper, but the light of Christ shines through the illuminated souls.

Gayatris

Pir

Inspirer of my mind, consoler of my heart, healer of my spirit,
Thy presence lifteth me from earth to heaven;
Thy words flow as the sacred river;
Thy thought riseth as a divine spring;
Thy tender feelings waken sympathy in my heart.
Beloved Teacher, thy very being is forgiveness.
The clouds of doubt and fear are scattered by thy piercing glance;
all ignorance vanishes in thy illuminating presence;
a new hope is born in my heart by breathing thy peaceful atmosphere.
O inspiring Guide, through life's puzzling ways,
in thee I feel abundance of blessing.

Nabi

A torch in the darkness, a staff during my weakness,
a rock in the weariness of life,
Thou, my Guide, makest earth a paradise.
Thy thought giveth me unearthly joy,
Thy light illuminateth my life's path,
Thy words inspire me with divine wisdom.
I follow in thy footsteps, which lead me to the eternal goal.
Comforter of the brokenhearted,
Support of those in need,
Friend of the lovers of Truth,
Blessed Guide, thou art the Prophet of God.

Rasul

Warner of coming dangers,
Wakener of the world from sleep,
Deliverer of the Message of God,
Thou art our Savior.
The Sun at the dawn of creation,
the Light of the whole universe,
the Fulfillment of God's Purpose,
Thou, the Life Eternal, we seek refuge in thy loving enfoldment.
Spirit of Guidance,
Source of all beauty, and Creator of harmony,
Love, Lover, and Beloved Sovereign.
Thou art our Divine Ideal.

Chalas

God and the devil are the two extreme poles of the ego; one represents perfection and the other limitation.

The moment one realizes when to speak and when to keep silence, one takes one's first step in the path of wisdom.

Living in the world without insight into the hidden laws of nature is like not knowing the language of the country in which one was born.

A continual pursuit after the impossible is the chronic disease of the human being.

Seeking after that which is beyond one's reach is the oil that feeds the flame of hope.

The surface of the human intelligence is the intellect; when it is turned outside in, it becomes the source of all revelation.

Nothing is impossible, all is possible; impossibility is only a boundary of limitation that stands around the human mind.

Facts lose their color in the face of Truth, as stars pale before the sun.

It is not difficult at all to please the saint, the saint can most easily be pleased; the difficulty is in pleasing the other, who is the opposite of the saint.

So few in this world discriminate properly between their want and their need.

A responsible person is worth more than a thousand people who labor.

It is true that the light of wisdom must continually be kept alight; but it is difficult always to act rightly.

Either you must pass from all things that interest you in this life upon earth or else they will pass you, for the very nature of this life on earth is changing.

Through every condition, agreeable or disagreeable, the soul makes its way toward the goal.

The lovers who lean upon the beloved's response, their love is like the flame that needs oil to live; but the lovers who stand on their own feet are like the lantern of the sun that burns without oil.

A simple statement often takes away the charm of something that may be left unsaid.

If people do not come up to your mark, do not become annoyed, but rejoice, knowing that your mark is high.

The sense of discretion is instinctive, and it is the life one lives that either shapes it or deforms it.

There is no gain without a sacrifice; if there be any, sacrifice must follow.

Are you looking for an ideal soul? Such a person has never been born. But if you still seek after such a person, then you will have to create one of your own imagination.

When you have learned all there is to be learned, then you will realize that there was nothing to be learned.

The moment a prisoner feels that they will no longer remain in the prison, the prison bars must break instantly of themselves.

Contentment raises one above the strife of worthless things and beyond the limitation of human nature.

It is seldom that too little is said and too much is done, but often the contrary.

The motive power is creative and constructive, yet it is motive that limits the power, which is limitless.

All pain is significant of change. All that changes, for better or worse, must cause a certain amount of pain, for change is at once birth and death.

All conventionality that has limited the life of a person and has removed it far from nature, comes from sex distinction.

People were sent into the artificial world that they may meet every conventionality, in which lies all tragedy of life.

One who lacks imagination and is of little faith is unable to tread the spiritual path.

Faith and imagination are wings of the bird that flies in the spiritual spheres.

If the owl of Sophia had been as wise as she, it would not have sat in her presence so spellbound.

Kindness that is not balanced with firmness may prove to be weakness.

People are not only ready to profit by your wisdom, power, and greatness, but they are also eager to take advantage of your ignorance, weakness, and inability.

Being able to trust others apart, if you have learned to trust yourself, you have accomplished something.

Every person has a place in life, and no one can hold a place long that is not their own.

By trying to look upon life not only from one's own point of view but also from the point of view of another, one loses nothing, but on the contrary widens the horizon of one's view.

To express an impulse gives relief, but to control it gives strength.

Perfection is attained by five achievements: life, light, power, happiness, and peace.

By creating happiness, one fulfills one's life's purpose.

If dogs bark at the elephant, it takes no notice and goes on its way; so do the wise, when attacked by the ignorant.

There are many wrong paths, but there is one right way that leads to the goal.

You will find reasons, whether you want to be pessimistic or optimistic, to support your view.

Seers distinguish between the real and the unreal until they arrive at a point where all to them becomes the reality.

When you do not concern yourself with the consequences, then alone you may freely express your impulse.

One cannot be wise and foolish at the same time, for light and darkness cannot be together.

Illuminated souls do not seek after occult powers, but occult powers, by themselves, come to them.

It is not the heart of the earth in which to confide, for it brings forth all that is given to it in simple trust; it is the soul of heaven that is trustworthy, for it assimilates all in its own being.

"Why?" is an animal with a thousand tails; every bite you give it, it drops one of its curved tails and raises another. Its hunger is never satisfied so long as its mouth is open.

Life is the longing of every soul; the one who seeks life through death becomes immortal.

Those whom you have lost here, you will find in some other place.

In the friendship, as well as in the hostility of the worldly, there is pain.

"Yesterday I was not wise enough, today I understand, tomorrow I will do better." So one thinks, and life goes on.

The prophet is the painter of the ideal that is beyond human comprehension.

What does it matter if Krishna was Christ or Abraham was Moses? One thing is true, that there was, there is, and there always will be a knower of God, a lover of souls, a server of humanity.

The person who tries to prove their belief superior to the faith of another does not know the meaning of religion.

When people argue over a problem, it does not always mean that they know it. Most often they argue because they want to complete their knowledge without admitting their ignorance.

The light illuminates the path of those who are distant from it; those who are near are dazzled by it.

There can be no comparison between art and nature, for art is as limited as the human being, but nature is as perfect as God.

Self-effacement does not in any way lessen, it only makes one limitless.

Duty is not necessarily the purpose of life; still in duty one finds a road that leads one to the purpose of life.

No sooner the God-ideal is brought to life, than the worshippers of God turn into Truth. Then Truth is no longer their seeking; Truth becomes their being, and in the light of that absolute Truth they find all knowledge.

It was not the Lord who was crucified; what was crucified was only his limitation.

If an idol made of rock is made God by its worshippers, why then should a personality not become divinity for the devotees?

The one who makes fun of another seldom knows that there is something laughable in them also.

Every person has their own reason; therefore two persons cannot always understand one another.

There is one thing to be said against the kindhearted, that they never can be kind enough.

Whether a small person loves you or hates you, in either case they will pull you down to their own level.

To delve into a matter that matters little is like raising dust from the ground.

It is belief that in its perfection becomes faith.

Even a plain thought gets tangled when told to the person who has a knot in their head.

When a thoughtful person risks falling at each step they take in the path of life, what about a thoughtless person?

Despair not if your friend has taken advantage of you, but be contented knowing that it was not your enemy.

There are habits that can best be prevented before one has formed them. Once you have taken to a habit, then it is difficult to give it up.

Rules of the world are different from the law of the path that mystics tread.

One who fights for justice in the affairs of this world may fight forever, for that one will never find it; justice is only manifest in the sum total of life.

When you stand on this earth and look at life there is all injustice and chaos everywhere; but when you rise above and look below it is all just and perfect and everything appears to be in its proper place.

When one arrives at God-knowledge from self-knowledge, one makes God as small as one's little self; but when one comes to self-knowledge through the knowledge of God, one becomes as large as God.

The supreme law is that all is just and all is right, but is this law to be proclaimed? No, it is to be understood.

The attribute is not important; it is the possessor of the attribute who is important.

If someone can discover with any authority the true source of happiness, he or she can find it only in pain.

Faith is the culmination of belief. It is that faith which is the mystery of life, the secret of salvation.

It is not evidence which gives belief. Belief that stands above evidence is that belief which, in the end, will culminate in faith.

Belief is the food of the believers, it is the sustenance of their faith; it is on belief that they live, not on food and water.

By learning to think one develops dignity in nature. The more one thinks, the more dignified one becomes, because dignity springs out of thoughtfulness.

Reason belongs to earth and heaven both, its depth is heavenly, its surface earthly; and that which fills the gap in the form of reason between heaven and earth is that middle part of it which unites it. Therefore reason can be most confusing, and reason can be most enlightening.

The reason one seeks for happiness is not because happiness is one's sustenance, but because happiness is one's own being; therefore in seeking for happiness one is seeking for oneself.

Religion is not in performing a ceremony or a ritual; true religion is the feeling or the sense of duty.

What virtue is that, O righteous person, which gives no happiness?

If you have lost something it means that you have either risen above it or fallen below it.

People expect another to place them in a higher position, but the place to which they are equal they take themselves.

The dead can give nothing living, nor can the living give anything dead.

It is better that your enemy stands before your house rather than that they should live under your roof.

White forces or dark forces, all will surrender to you with the waxing of the moon of your life; but in the waning moon they will show their influence.

It matters little whether you are on the top of the mountain or at the foot of it, if you are happy where you are.

If you feel your thoughts, your thoughts will become your being.

The ones who are not moved to dance by the movements of an innocent babe have not yet risen from their graves.

One cannot praise God unless one makes of God an ideal.

Watching with interest the winning ways of a little child is a wonderful lovemaking.

Every thing and every being is placed in its own place in life, and each is busy carrying out that work that has to be done in the whole scheme of nature.

A religious ritual, for a spiritual person, is but a recreation.

To find appropriate words to express an idea is more complicated than painting a picture.

Destiny can take your best friend as an instrument to cause you harm, and your worst enemy to do you good.

Power is best utilized when it is used for a good purpose.

If one lacks understanding one is poor with all the good of this world one possesses; it is understanding that is the true riches.

The one who complains about everything certainly has a complaint somewhere in his or her head.

One exaltation I have called sensation, the other I have called exaltation. Sensation gives pleasure, exaltation gives happiness.

No sooner you begin to see the bad side of a person's character, you automatically put a cover over the good side of their nature.

A person, however great, must not claim perfection; for the blind world can only see the limitation of their external being.

There are some souls who, if you do not make them your friends, will become your enemies.

The one who wants to become a master must first pass through an examination as a servant.

God cannot be good and perfect at the same time; it takes good and bad both to make perfection.

Fools are not entitled to know the mystery that the wise are supposed to possess.

The knowledge of truth is not enough; in order to impart it to others, one must know the psychology of human nature.

The purpose of life is fulfilled in rising to the greatest heights and in diving to the deepest depths of life.

Peace will not come to a lover's heart so long as that one will not become love itself.

All things pertaining to spiritual progress in life depend upon peace.

The most beautiful form of the love of God is God's compassion, God's divine forgiveness.

NIRTAN

The Dance of the Soul

Alankara: The fanciful expression of an idea.

Bola: A great idea in a few burning words.

Chala: A definite statement.

Gamaka: What comes from the heart of the poet, resisting the attempt to keep it back, keyed to various notes.

Sura: God speaking through the kindled soul.

Tala: A rhythm formed by comparison.

Tana: The soul speaking with nature.

Alankaras

Thou changest thy place, but not thyself, O Light.

Unfold Thy secret through nature and reveal Thy mystery through my heart.

Let me become Thy body, Thou become my spirit, O Holy One.

Let the sun of the Thy divine spirit rise from my heart, that morn may break out of the darkness of life.

I shall penetrate through the black heart of the clouds to reach Thee, my Liege.

My life is a wave of the ocean of Thy eternal life.

Let my life become Thy soul; let my soul become Thy life.

Through the darkness of night my soul seeks for Thee.

Warn me, God, through Thy Prophet, before I step into error.

Divinity I see in Thy spirit of Risalat.

Thine own ideal I see in the perfection of Rasul.

I hold ear to the depth of Thy blessing when the storm breaks through life's sea.

Let me recognize Thy visage in the image of Thy Avatar.

My heart is no more mine, it is thine own, my spiritual guide.

Heal my soul through the inspiring glance of Thy Messiah.

O your rising waves of favor,
and your raging flames of wrath,
on the rose they are like dewdrops,
on the flame just like the moth.

I see thy spirit, O Rasul, under the veil of my spiritual guide.

The dark clouds brought romance between Thee, my Beloved, and me.

Let my heart reflect the spirit of the Holy Ones.

Let my self turn into Thy Being.

My vanity! It amuses me to see thee dance at the sight of my limitation.

The rapture of my heart shows the mark of Thy lips.

Let Thy perfection be mine and my imperfection be lost as the darkness in the full moon.

My heart! At times one moment is as a year, and at times one year is as a moment to thee.

Heaven: I cry and shed tears when clouds gather round my heart, and when the light of my soul is covered from my sight.

The soul: Mother's arms receive me when I come to the earth, and Father's arms lift me up at the moment when I return.

Heart

Heart hath its head on its own palm,
Face of the heart is veiled.
Heart's hands are tied with iron chains,
Feet of the heart are nailed.

Eyes of the heart are never dry,
Heart speaks only through tears.
Ears of the heart are so keen
That voice from the distance it hears.

Voice of the heart is silent,
Yet far-reaching is heart's cry.
Heart hath no question nor answer,
Heart is expressed in deep sigh.

Ways of the heart are mysterious,
Though heart hath mind of a child.
Heart's breath is full of tenderness,
And heart's expression is mild.

Ideal alone is heart's deity,
Constant yearning its life.
Heart's not concerned with life or death,
Heart stands firm through all strife.

Beauty is heart's only object,
Its inspirer, its all.
Heart is all power that there is,
Angels attend heart's call.

Heart is itself its own medicine,
Heart all its own wounds heals.
No one can ever imagine
The pain the loving heart feels.

Path of the heart is thorny,
Which leads in the end to bliss.
Hope is the staff heart holds in hand,
Heart's one desire is a kiss.

Truth

Face of the Truth is open,
Eyes of Truth are bright;
Lips of the Truth are ever closed,
Head of the Truth is upright.

Words of the Truth are touching,
Voice of the Truth is deep;
Law of the Truth is simple,
All that you sow, you reap.

Soul of the Truth is flaming,
Heart of the Truth is warm;
Mind of the Truth is clear and firm
Through the rain or storm.

Life of the Truth is eternal,
Immortal is its past;
Power of Truth will endure,
Truth holds good to the last.

Chest of the Truth stands forward,
Gaze of the Truth is straight;
Truth hath no fear nor hath doubt,
Truth hath patience to wait.

Facts are all shadows, and
Truth stands above all sin;
Great in life be the battle,
Truth in the end will win.

Image of the Truth is Christ,
Sacred word its rod;
Sign of Truth is the cross,
And soul of the Truth is God.

Suras

There is no reason that one must know God because one is born on earth; it is only the birth of one's soul that makes one entitled to that knowledge.

Life is reality, death is its shadow; but as the shadow is seen and yet nonexistent, so is death.

Death opens a door between life here and hereafter.

Death is a silent voyage to the port of eternity.

Death is no more death to those who have once experienced its sting.

Death is but the turning of a page of life.

To the eyes of others it is death, but to those who die it is life.

Tanas

Glorious sun, are you setting?
Yes, to rise again.

Sublime nature, my ears did not hear your music.
Your heart has heard it, your soul has danced to it.

Trees to the clouds: "With raised hands we pay you our homage."
Clouds in tears: "I grant your request."

Nature, where do you borrow your sublimity?
From your loving spirit.

Rain, why do you not come in the desert?
I keep away from where I am not welcome.

When once passing through the mountains, I saw rocks, some sitting on their knees, some bending, some standing.

I asked: "O hard-hearted monsters, what secret is there in your charm?"

They answered in a silent voice: "Because we do not assert ourselves."

Rocky mountains, what are you?
We are the tombs of the world's past.

Crystal, what are you?
I am a shadow of Christ's heart.
What quality do you possess?
I am empty of self, so that by gazing one sees in me his heart reflected.

Glorious nature, wonderful picture, where shall I keep you?
In the frame of your heart.

Desert to the clouds: "You are passing over us, why not be our guest?"
We no longer have trust in the hard-hearted.

Wilderness, why does your cry touch me so deeply?
Because it rises from the bottom of my heart.

Wilderness, what is in you that is so overwhelming?
The expansion of my heart.

Goodbye, nature's vision, shall I ever see you again?
Yes, whenever you will open the album of your heart.

Gamakas

Why was I born, God, if not to find Thee? Why do I die, God, if not to come to Thee?

When the unreality of life pushes against my heart, its door opens to the reality.

The past was my dream, the present is my play, the future will be my plan.

I am the one who is perfected by heaven, limited by the earth, and expected by humanity who knows me not.

Can anyone break me? No, by doing so, one may as well prepare to break God. Neither can I be broken nor God; but the one who wishes to break, alone will be broken.

I draw all my strength from my humility.

A tongue of flame rises from every wound of my heart, illuminating my path through life and guiding my way to the goal.

The rapidity of my walk imagination cannot follow.

People ask me questions that I cannot put in words; it gives me discomfort when they cannot hear the voice of my silence.

By every hurt or harm that one causes me only makes me know that one better.

I came as I was made to come, I live as life allows me to live, but I will be what I wish to be.

With every pinprick a drop of blood comes out of my heart, and that drop becomes the wine of sacrament.

I have not come to teach those who consider themselves teachers; I have come to learn from the teachers and to teach my pupils.

When my heart is perturbed it upsets the whole universe.

When my heart is asleep, both the worlds slumber.

The whole creation wakens with the wakening of my heart.

When my heart breaks, pearls become scattered around.

My heart attains self-sufficiency by eating its own flesh and drinking its own blood.

I tremble at the sight of the task that hath been given me, and I feel out of breath when I weigh my ideal with my limitation

Worldly success to me is like a doll's wedding.

I am the wine of the holy sacrament, my mere presence is intoxicating; those who will keep sober after drinking my cup will be illuminated; but those who will not assimilate it will expose themselves to the ridicule of the world.

My heart drinks its own tears and puts them out as pearls.

I prefer failure to success gained by falsehood.

The true exaltation comes to me from the insults I have to endure in life, rather than from the respectful attitude of my murids.

Many underestimate the greatness of the Cause seeing the limitation through which I have to work my way out.

The Message is a call to those whose hour has come to awake, and a lullaby to those who are still meant to sleep.

How can a person claim to be a world teacher and be sane at the same time?

The essence of today's message is balance.

You are my life, it is in you that I live;
From you I borrow life, and you do I give.
O you, my soul and spirit, you I adore;
I live in you, so do I live evermore.
You are in me and in you do I live;
Still you are my king and my sins you forgive.
You are the present and the future and past;
I lost my self but I have found you at last.

Why, O my feeling heart
do you live and die?
What makes my feeling heart
now to laugh and then to cry?
Death is my life indeed,
I live when I die.
Pain is my pleasure;
when I laugh then I cry.

Some did say that I knew nothing,
Some still held that I knew all.
Some did turn their back to me, and

Some quickly answered my call.
Some on hearing my words exclaimed,
"Nothing he said that was new."
Some said, "I have always thought this,
This is my own point of view."
Some asked what mystery he revealed,
What wonder did he perform?
Some answered, "We ask no wonder
So long as his heart is warm."
Some said, "He's a man as we are;
What difference in him do you see?"
Some answered, "It is not to know;
What is needed is to be."

Before you judge my actions,
Lord, I pray, you will forgive.
Before my heart has broken,
Will you help my soul to live?

Before my eyes are covered,
Will you let me see your face?
Before my feet are tired,
May I reach your dwelling place?

Before I wake from slumber,
You will watch me, Lord, I hold.
Before I throw my mantle,
Will you take me in your fold?

Before my work is over,
You, my Lord, will right the wrong.
Before you play your music,
Will you let me sing my song?

Bolas

The saints are forgiveness itself.

In the influence that controls a situation, the hand of God is seen.

The more one can bear, the more one is given to bear.

If one wants to know life, one can know it best by one's own life.

No beloved has ever known the depth of the lover's heart.

Sometimes success is a defeat and defeat is a success.

One unconsciously pays happiness in order to buy pleasure.

Life is interesting with friends and enemies both.

All difficult things are made easy by willingness.

Give not nor claim love by force, for love is an affair of mutual willingness.

Silence is an unadmitting consent and an uncommitting refusal.

Walking on the turning wheel of the earth, living under the ever-rotating sun, a person expects a peaceful life.

To discover the heart is the greatest initiation.

A consent after refusing is worse than a refusal.

One's own self has the right to accuse one's self for one's faults, rather than anyone else.

Truth is born of falsehood, as light cometh from darkness.

A charming personality is more precious than all wealth.

Mystics perfect themselves by making themselves empty of themselves.

Sorrow enables a person to experience joy.

The Creator, by means of the human heart, experiences life within and without.

Tears of joy are more precious than pearls.

If you avoid wrongdoing, it will avoid you.

A real artist expresses their soul in their art.

Simplicity is not always interesting.

Divinity is the exaltation of the human soul.

It is not the action that is sin, it is the attitude of mind that makes it.

Silence speaks louder than words.

Reality unfolds with the breaking of the heart.

Christ is God reduced and the human enlarged.

The vision of nature is the presence of God.

In the heart of sorrow there is a seed of joy.

The house is built with matter but made with spirit.

Righteousness gives strength, and falseness weakens the mind.

No one would do wrong if he or she knew the wrong of it.

Love in giving and taking is commercialized. It is in its pure essence when love is for its own joy.

The spirit of feeling is lost when a sentiment is expressed in words.

Retire from the mundane things of life as much as life would permit you.

Avoid all nonsense.

Accomplishment is more valuable than what is accomplished.

Life is time, and death is its division.

We need not tolerate inharmony, but we may act indifferent to it.

It is the separation that is separated, not we.

One who gives love will receive a thousandfold in return.

Evil is like shadow.

Nature is born, character is built, and personality is developed.

Time and space, therefore, are the hands and the feet of the mystics. Through space they climb and through time they accomplish.

A person seeks freedom, and pursues captivity.

Perfection is to be found in looking for one, in pursing one, in finding one, in realizing one.

Talas

Befool not, O night, the morn will break;
Beware, O darkness, the sun will shine;
Be not vain, O mist, it will once be clear;
Forget not, my sorrow, once joy will arise.

A labor done without wages,
a service without thanks,
a merit without appreciation,
a love without answer,
have a different value to them.

If you are annoyed by any disagreeable experience, it is a loss; but if you have learnt by it, it is a gain.

It does not matter how hard you labor, it is what you accomplish that counts.

The birds, creatures with wings, will never have a lasting attachment with the animals; so it is even with people. The wayfarer of the heavens can never keep attached to the dweller of the earth.

Sweeter than honey are the results of one's toil,
more fragrant than flowers are the words of praise,
more delicious than fruit is an obedient child,
more precious than a pearl is a congenial mate.

Impulse's intoxicating action is absorbing, but it is the result of every deed that brings a person to realization.

By pessimism you miss the chance of gaining. By optimism you take the chance of losing.

When you care for the opinion of others, you are below them; when you do not care, you are above them.

Chalas

Raise not dust from the ground, it will enter in your eyes. Sprinkle some water on it that it may settle down and lie under your feet.

Pick not flowers, for it will detain you in your progress on the path; and as you go they will only fade away. Look at them, therefore, and admire their beauty; and as you proceed in your journey they will greet you with smiles all along the way.

Glossary

alankara: Ornament, decoration; a fanciful expression of an idea

alapa: Dialogue, prelude to a song; modulation of the voice in singing; God speaking to human, the principle theme of the Message; extemporization, a divine word in the form of advice

bola: Speech, tune; a kindled word, the words of a song; a great idea in a few burning words

chala: Agitation, motion, tune; an illuminated word; theme, a definite statement

gamaka: Convincing, showing; sound of the kettle drum; a violent clash in music; a deep tone, sound of a musical instrument; what comes from the heart of the poet, resisting the attempt to keep it back, keyed to various notes

gayan: Singer, singing, a song, a chant

gayatri: A sacred verse from the Rig Veda recited as a prayer; the name of a Vedic meter, a triplet of three divisions of eight syllables each; prayers, sacred chants

khatum: Conclusion, end

murid: Follower, disciple of a murshid

murshid: Guide, spiritual teacher, head of religious order

nabi: Prophet, the degree below rasul

nayaz: Petition, prayer

nazar: Vow, gift, offering

nirtan: Dance

pir: Holy person, saint, spiritual guide

raga: A mode in music, song; love, affection, desire; the human soul calling upon the beloved God; modulation, the outpouring of the soul

rasul: Messenger, prophet; the highest degree of the spiritual hierarchy

risalat: Prophethood

salat: Prayer, blessing, benediction, service; the first duty of a Muslim

saum: Literally "fasting," but also renunciation, abstaining, surrender to the divine

sura: Degree, step; air, tune; God speaking through the kindled soul; a note

tala: Clapping of hands, rhythm, musical time or measure; the rhythmic expression of an idea; a rhythm formed by comparison

tana: Tension, musical tone, keynote, trill ; the soul speaking with nature

vadan: Playing on musical instruments; musical symphony

Hazrat Pir-o-Murshid Inayat Khan

Biographical Note

Hazrat Inayat Khan was born in Baroda, India, in 1882. Trained in Hindustani classical music from childhood, he became a professor of music at an early age. In the course of extensive travels in the Indian subcontinent, he won high acclaim at the courts of the maharajas and received the title of Tansen-uz-Zaman from the Nizam of Hyderabad.

In Hyderabad Hazrat Inayat Khan became the disciple of Sayyid Abu Hashim Madani, who trained him in the traditions of the Chishti, Suhrawardi, Qadiri, and Naqshbandi lineages of Sufism, and at last blessed him to "Fare forth into the world."

In 1910, accompanied by his brother Maheboob Khan and cousin Mohammed Ali Khan, Hazrat Inayat Khan sailed for the United States. Over the next sixteen years he traveled and taught widely throughout the United States and Europe, building up the first Sufi order ever established in the West.

In London Hazrat Inayat Khan married Ora Ray Baker. They raised their four children in London during the First World War and afterward in Suresnes, France, where a little Sufi village sprang up around their home, Fazal Manzil.

The doors of Hazrat Inayat Khan's Sufi Order, known today as the Inayatiyya, were open to people of all faiths. Appealing to experience rather than belief, Hazrat Inayat Khan's discourses and spiritual instructions illuminated the twin themes of the presence of God in the depths of the human soul and the interconnectedness of all people. Numerous books were compiled from Hazrat Inayat Khan's teachings during his lifetime and posthumously. In September 1926 Hazrat Inayat Khan bade farewell to his family and disciples and returned to India. On February 5, 1927, he died and was buried in New Delhi.

Index

A

B

C

D

E

F

G

Q

R

S

Y

Z

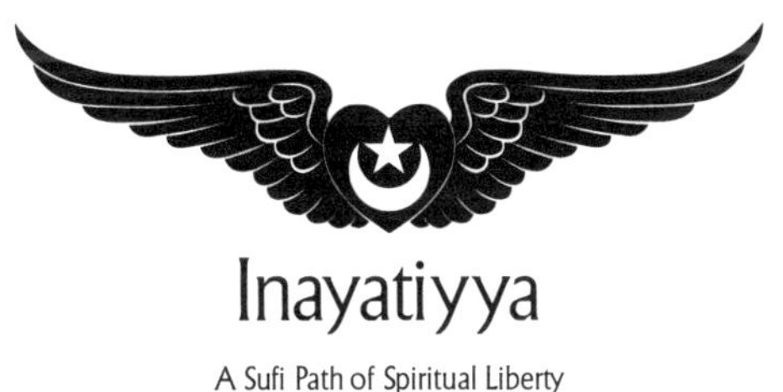

Sulūk Press is an independent publisher dedicated to issuing works of spirituality and cultural moment, with a focus on Sufism, in particular, the works of Hazrat Inayat Khan and his successors. To learn more about Inayatiyya Sufism, please visit **inayatiyya.org**.